I0032151

Customer F.I.R.S.T.

Managing customers and
suppliers to deliver
professional, responsive
service - every time.

ISBN 978-0-9868718-1-8 "Customer F.I.R.S.T." Copyright (C) 2018, Brent Finnamore Second Edition

All rights reserved. No part of this book may be reproduced or transmit- ted in any form or by any means, electronic or mechanical, including photocopying, recording or by any information storage and retrieval system without express permission from Brent Finnamore.

"Customer F.I.R.S.T.", "T.E.A.M.S.", "Can-Sandwich" and "H.E.A.T." are trademarks of The Finnamore Group Inc.

About the Author

As president of The Finnamore Group Inc. Brent leverages his 25+ years of deep knowledge in customer service best practices to help companies improve their customer experience and drive sales.

Since receiving his education from the University of New Brunswick in 1993 Brent has delivered consulting, coaching, training and keynotes to more than 370,000 people in hundreds of companies, in dozens of industries, around the globe.

Brent helps companies transform their human and organizational capital into tangible business results. Working with the leadership and front-line teams of his clients, Brent helps companies improve sales results, customer service performance and culture change.

Residing in Montreal, Canada, Brent is an avid Ironman triathlete and marathon runner (avid, not fast!).

You are welcome to contact Brent to find out how he can help your organization or read more of his insights:

brent.finnamore@thefinnamoregroup.com

www.thefinnamoregroup.com
http://brentfinnamore.wordpress.com

What is Your Company's Most Valuable Asset?

It seems like an innocent enough question, "What is your organization's most valuable asset?" Yet the answers we get in our classes and consultations are never quite complete.

"The most valuable asset in your company is your customer - but ONLY if they are being satisfied, profitably, by empowered, engaged employees, who are working with sustainable processes."

Any surprises there? Would you have said, *"The most valuable asset in my company is people?"* But what if you have great people and no customers? What if you have lousy products? Would you have said, *"The most valuable asset is our technology/intellectual property?"* But what if you can't scale to serve your customers? What if you're losing money as you serve them? The answer we gave you above probably makes intuitive sense, but it comes with a catch – it must include every element in order to be true. Your customer is your most valuable asset only if you are able to serve them under the conditions we outlined. And that requires your company to be just about perfect.

The great news, perhaps, is that even in the absence of any of the conditions stated above, the tools and skills outlined in this book will still help you provide a better customer experience. In fact, many of the tools and skills you'll discover in this book are actually designed with the idea that no one works in a perfect company.

Let's begin our journey to customer service excellence by defining three important groups of people which are fundamental to the techniques and principles of this book: Customers, suppliers and colleagues.

Definition of a Customer:

A customer is anyone (external or internal to your organization) who needs something from you in order to perform their role.

By this definition anyone can be your customer and everyone has a customer. Customers are the people or groups that are the recipients or benefactors of your work output. Customers can be colleagues, departments, companies or governments. When someone needs some- thing from you (information, approval, solutions, products, documents, ideas, etc.) then in those moments they are your customer and you are their supplier. Some service cycles take months, while others take seconds.

Definition of a Supplier:

A supplier is anyone (external or internal to your organization) you need something from in order to perform your role.

By this definition anyone can be your supplier and everyone has a supplier. Suppliers are the people or groups whose outputs help you perform your role. When you need something from someone (information, approval, solutions, products, documents, ideas, etc.) then in those moments they are your supplier and you are their customer.

It may seem like no other definitions are necessary - you have customers and suppliers, simple. But not every relationship can be neatly fitted into these two concepts. Some relationships are more complex than these two basic concepts describe.

Definition of a Colleague/Partner:

A colleague or partner is anyone (external or internal to your organization) with whom you exchange value.

Many people with whom you interact do not fit neatly into the customer or supplier definitions, even though those definitions are broad. Imagine you work for an app-based company. Perhaps you can say that your Users are customers, but what about your advertisers or your shareholders? Are they customers? Are they suppliers? Really, they are neither. They are strategic partners; they are colleagues. Colleagues can be board members, co-workers, shareholders, managers, employees, strategic partners, and of course any colleague at any time can be either a customer or a supplier, depending on the interaction. This nuance matters because even if someone is not clearly a customer or a supplier, they still need your help and you still need theirs.

It is to these three groups of people that we will be applying the tools and skills in this book. In other words, to everyone.

The Two Pillars of World-Class Service

To satisfy your customers, suppliers and colleagues - and to satisfy your external customers profitably - everyone in the value stream must excel at one thing which is really two things:

Do the right thing, and do it the right way. One is technical, the other is interpersonal.

Technical - Do the right things. In order to be a company that provides *good* customer service everyone must be technically excellent. Your technical knowledge, experience and problem-solving skills enable you to provide customers with accurate information and correct solutions. They allow you to permanently resolve issues as quickly as possible, and in as few steps as possible. Technical excellence requires technical knowledge, financial knowledge, customer knowledge, company knowledge, the ability to diagnose problems and prescribe correct solutions.

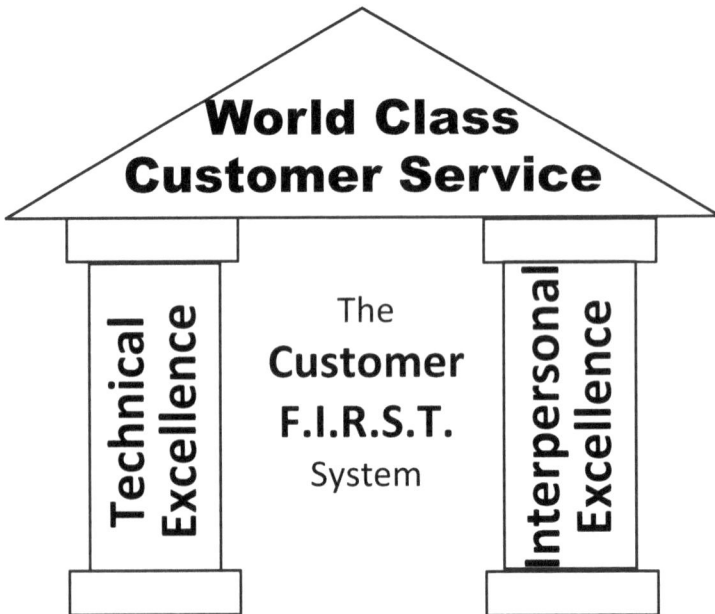

Interpersonal - Do them the right way. In order to be a company that provides *good* customer service everyone must be interpersonally excellent. You must become a master of the interaction itself. In addition to excellent technical service, customers desire a positive interpersonal experience. What if you're a technical wizard but you come across to the customer as apathetic, argumentative, condescending, or arrogant? If you solve a problem but create discomfort or stress in the process, you have not served the customer well. Similarly of course, if you handle the customer effectively but provide inaccurate information or make other preventable mistakes you have not served the customer well. Interpersonal excellence requires a positive, professional attitude, respectfulness, empathy, responsiveness, diplomacy, assertiveness and the ability to subtly control both your customers and suppliers using the subtle skills of influence.

Technical and interpersonal excellence. In order to be a company that provides *world-class* customer service, everyone must have both. This book focuses on interpersonal excellence during interactions with customers, suppliers and colleagues. The Customer F.I.R.S.T. system itself, in fact, is designed for just that purpose: To help you leverage your technical skills with interpersonal excellence.

The Customer F.I.R.S.T. System

Customer F.I.R.S.T. is a set of interaction instructions that help to ensure a positive customer experience every time.

Feel good, and help your customers feel good (valued, respected, informed, assured and trusting).

Identify the need or opportunity and Receive the *right* information and context.

Send the *right* message (the right commitment and the right options), and manage expectations.

Take the *right* action with colleagues and suppliers to deliver highly reliable options.

The F.I.R.S.T. system can and should be used by *everyone* in the company but is particularly helpful for people who interact with external customers. You can use this system to produce higher quality results as you interact with internal and external customers, suppliers and colleagues - either by phone, email, virtual meetings or face-to-face.

The system has been honed by our team over the past twenty years with thousands of service professionals in dozens of industries to help you and your team:

- Effectively manage customers - both in normal and in escalated situations.

- Effectively manage difficult customers and difficult situations that may involve both customers and suppliers.

- Manage urgency and reduce the need to expedite/rush unnecessarily, while still being timely and responsive to customers.

- Ensure commitments are consistently met throughout value streams.

- Educate customers and create realistic expectations which help allow your company to deliver on promises more consistently.

- Successfully persuade your customers, suppliers and colleagues to do what you need them to do (in the case of your external customers, this can often be essential for them to get great service from your organization).

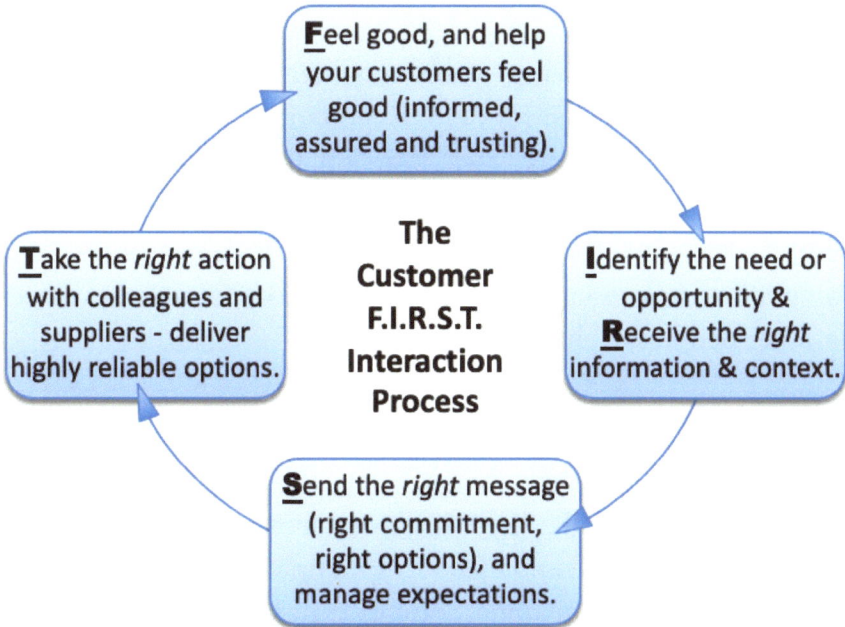

Key Behavioral Competencies of Customer F.I.R.S.T.

It's helpful to think of the F.I.R.S.T. system as a set of behavioral competencies. A behavioral competency is a series of behaviors that work together in synergy to produce predictable, professional, consistent, efficient flow of value throughout the various segments of supply chains – to your end-customer. Competencies are the actually the product of three elements: Knowledge, skills and talent. Knowledge and skills are teachable; talent is not.

Knowledge

There are two kinds of knowledge - both are technical in nature: Factual and experiential. Factual knowledge means knowing your products, services, methodologies and systems. It also means knowing your organizational structure and resources - where to go for help. Experiential knowledge means the wisdom that comes from time on the job. For example, knowing which people in the contracts department are the most helpful, knowing a workaround for the repair process of a component, or knowing that it's always risky to make promises on other peoples' behalf.

Skills

Knowledge is important, but it's just the start. Skills are the how-to's and methods for doing your work well. Skills allow you to *apply* your knowledge. Examples of skills include calming an angry customer down, building trust, managing expectations, making reliable commitments, and overcoming resistance from others when you make requests.

Talent

Talent is the final, "secret" ingredient that sparks high performance in any behavioral competency. It involves your personality traits. Talent is the things about you that you couldn't change even if you wanted to - applied to the right role. They are your unrelenting nature. Walt Disney famously said, "We finally figured out that you can't train people to be friendly; you have to hire friendly people and then train them to be good at their jobs." Friendliness is not a teachable skill - it is a talent. Your personality traits determine the things you naturally strive for in your work and life – those are your talents. Just how *useful* your talent is to an organization, however, is also a function of your skills and your knowledge, both of which are learnable.

The many studies done on superior service performance reveal three types of great service professionals: The friendly director, the amiable administrator, and the assertive doer. The talents that describe each of these three types are outlined below.

Type 1- Friendly Director:

Friendly Directors are driven (motivated and yet methodical) and agreeable (accommodating and friendly). As a result of these two talents, they are empathetic and helpful, but they are also detail-oriented and seek to methodically resolve customer issues. They like to see things through, they follow reliable procedures, and they like to keep organized. Customers like them because they are pleasant to interact with and they can always provide accurate updates on the current service issue. Customers also like how they keep track of details. It signals to them that the Friendly Director is competent.

Type 2 – Amiable Administrator:

Amiable Administrators are agreeable (accommodating and friendly), but rather than being driven, they are spontaneous (flexible and freewheeling). As a result, they are not as detail-oriented and disciplined as Friendly Directors but are still very friendly and empathetic, and also possess a high need to help and serve others. Because they are not as disciplined as other types, their style tends toward more of a reactive or administrative role. They are less proactive, and often less on-top-of-things. Customers like them, however, because their lack of "insistence on a process" can make them seem more accommodating. Whereas a Friendly director might say, "Here's your answer," the less prepared Amiable Administrator says, "Sure, I'd be happy to look into that for you."

Type 3- Assertive Doer:

Assertive Doers are driven, innovative, extroverted and solution-oriented. They are, according to research, the best type of customer service professional possible. In escalated situations, they innovate solutions on the spot and actively see them through to the last detail. They build and maintain collaborative networks so they always know who to talk to for help. They pay no attention to borders and boundaries when solving non-routine problems; they just go wherever they need to, and they don't stop until they get what they need. Customers love them because they quickly get to the point, and they make important things happen – fast. Interestingly, they are not always the most empathetic or friendly of the three types. But in many industries, customers don't value empathy without good solutions; they value good solutions, period.

All three elements - knowledge, skills and talent - are required for a competency. You may possess a specific talent but lack the knowledge or skills needed to apply that talent well. Similarly, you may possess the knowledge and skills needed in a role but lack the talent needed to perform the role with distinction.

Research supports the assertion that talent – something which cannot be taught – is more important to performance than knowledge or skills. All three are essential, but their contribution weight is not equal. But don't be discouraged if you think you may lack some of these talents. You can make *small* adjustments to your traits - and often those small adjustments are enough.

Let's look at the F.I.R.S.T. system again, but this time in the language of behavioral competencies.

Competency 1: Feeling Good, and helping your customers feel good (valued, respected, informed, assured and trusting).

- Creating and maintaining a positive, solution-focused attitude all day long.
- Delivering helpful, responsive service.
- Showing empathy, concern, and a sense of urgency.
- Building and maintaining trust.
- Displaying interpersonal behaviors that cause customers to trust you and cause suppliers to support you.

Competency 2: Identifying the need or opportunity and **Receiving** the right information and context.

- Ensuring compete, valid and current information.
- Asking well-designed questions to reveal more information about the customer's needs.

Competency 3: Sending the right message (the right commitment and the right options) and managing expectations.

- Checking capacity..
- Making highly reliable commitments.
- Educating customers to align expectations with capacity.
- Delivering potentially unpleasant news.

- Handling upset customers and their complaints.

Competency 4: Taking the right actions with colleagues and suppliers to deliver highly reliable options.

- Using clear, precise language to make requests and offer commitments.
- Creating a sense of urgency with colleagues and suppliers.
- Building reliable plans of action with gates and dates.
- Working with unreliable suppliers and colleagues to increase service levels.
- Verifying the degree and nature of the urgency.
- Developing Plan-B's in case of problems.
- Building & maintaining relationships.
- Connecting requests with priorities and concerns.
- Framing requests to align with the priorities of others.
- Overcoming objections and resistance.

Competency 5: Getting the Right Things Done (A Supplement to Customer F.I.R.S.T.)

- Establishing key outputs and priorities.
- Scheduling for maximum efficiency.
- Anticipating deliverables and being proactive.
- Handling scheduling conflicts.
- Controlling email and maximizing email effectiveness.
- Dealing with distractions and walk-ins.

Competency 1:

Feeling Good, and helping your customers feel good (valued, respected, informed, assured and trusting).

In my training classes I like to ask people to stand up, get a partner, and have one person in each pair lift a leg. I ask them, "Are you more stable or less? Are you harder to upset or easier? How hard are you working to keep your balance? How long could you sustain this effort? All day?" Then I get their partners to give them a nudge. They lose balance immediately. Then I get them to lower their leg and take a solid position while their partner gives them the same nudge as before. Nothing happens. I conclude, "When you're high-leg, little things upset you, but when you're balanced those same things don't." High-leg means feeling lousy or stressed - annoyed, irritated, frustrated, upset, angry, bothered, confused, insulted, overworked, under-appreciated, etc. Just like feeling good, feeling lousy comes in a wide variety of flavors.

Across all cultures, people who feel good tend to produce good results in their work and life while people who feel lousy - or high-leg - tend to produce lousy results. Research (S. Kramer, T. Amabile, HBR, Vol. 89, No. 5, May 2011, p 70-80) shows that people who report having 75% or more "good-mood" days make 76% more progress and experience 13% fewer setbacks than those who report fewer good days. They are also 46% more likely to find catalysts to achieving their projects and tasks. Those who experience more bad moods reported encountering more hindrances, fewer catalysts and making less progress – even in the same departments with same bosses as their good-mood colleagues.

Serving customers well means more than just addressing their issues and meeting their needs; it means having a positive interpersonal experience throughout the service cycle. That's hard to do when you're feeling high-leg. People who actively manage their moods by thinking in ways that cause them to feel good are better able to help customers feel good as they serve them. When you feel good you behave differently than when you feel negative or stressed; you are more polite, more patient, more empathetic, more willing to go the extra mile and you are more resourceful. You tend to make others feel valued, respected and important. When you are high-leg you are more likely to be impatient, curt, sarcastic, lazy, unhelpful, rude, dismissive and apathetic.

But of course, feeling good is not that simple in the real world. Our life circumstances, age, health, finances, relationships and job satisfaction can all influence how we feel on any given day. While some of these elements can often be changed, doing so can be slow and require a great deal of investment of time and energy. And there's more: Scientists from London, Harvard, San Diego and Zurich have shown that feeling good even has a genetic component. In their report, "Genes, Economics and Happiness," they conclude that almost a third of the variation in human happiness is heritable. Jan-Emmanuel DeNeuve, London school of Economics, looked at the gene that involves serotonin transport and how it affects happiness. Those with the long allele where 8% more likely than those with none to report high levels of happiness. Those with two long alleles where 17% more likely.

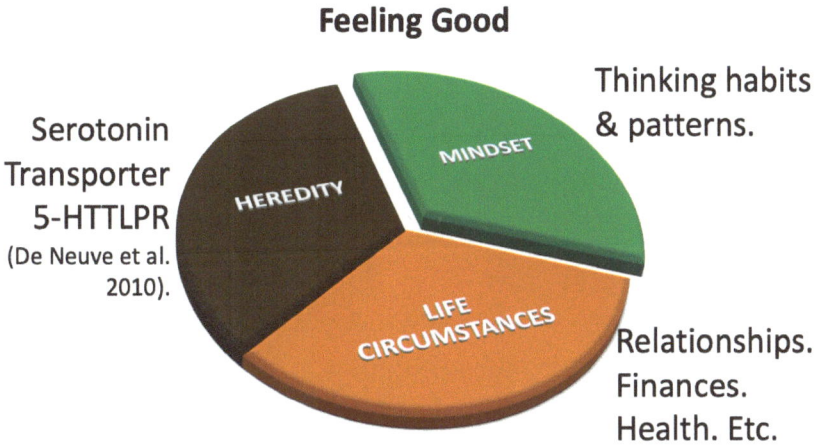

Feeling Good

Thinking habits & patterns.

MINDSET

Serotonin Transporter 5-HTTLPR
(De Neuve et al. 2010).

HEREDITY

LIFE CIRCUMSTANCES

Relationships. Finances. Health. Etc.

What can we make of all this? Your happiness is affected by three elements: 1) Heredity, which you can do nothing about, 2) Your life circumstances, which you can change but progress can be slow and expensive in terms of time and energy, and 3) Your thinking habits. It is in number three that we find the leverage we need. How you feel can largely be managed by your thinking habits. This is precious information. The two key components of our thinking habits are focus and perspective. Together they create our attitudes. Let's look at each one.

Focus refers to the things we choose to pay attention to, and therefore dwell on. Some people focus on what they don't like, what they don't want, what they don't have, on what could go wrong and how awful that would be. What kind of mood would that create? Try this little experiment: Don't think about your breathing. Do not think about your breathing. What are you thinking about? Your breathing. When you say to yourself, "I sure hope I don't have a lousy day," or, "I sure hope the customer doesn't get upset when I tell him this bad news," good luck. Our minds ignore the "don't" command, so if you think about what you don't want, you are likely to experience it anyway. Focus also affects what we *don't* notice. People who focus on what they don't have tend not to notice what they do have. Those who focus on what could go wrong usually are oblivious to opportunities to turn a situation around. People who always dwell on how badly things are broken can rarely help create good solutions. Some people believe it's their duty to point out to others how bad things are in their company. But in fact, those people are only doing half their job. Once you see something that needs improvement, then next step is to generate practical suggestions to close the gap in a positive, helpful way.

Do you focus on your customer's rude behavior or on the problem they're having that is causing the behavior? Do you focus on what you like about your job or what you don't like? Do you focus on what you don't want to happen or on what you want to have happen? Practice focusing deliberately on what you want, what you have, what you like, what you want to experience and how you can help make things better.

Perspective refers to the meaning we choose to make up about the things that happen to us. Human beings are meaning-makers. All day every day we make up meanings about things that happen to us and around us. The skill is to make up meanings that empower you and inspire you - and at the very least, meanings that don't leave you chronically angry, depressed or discouraged.

What does it mean when a customer is yelling at you through the phone? You could decide it means he is an unreasonable, childish, rude person. But how do you feel as a result of inventing that meaning? Do you feel like helping him and going the extra mile? On the other hand, you could decide it means he's crying for help; that he's a good person having a very bad day and he needs you to turn it around for him. From this perspective, you feel more like helping him. In both cases, the event is exactly the same. The only difference is what you do between your ears. Try to avoid making up meanings that cause you to become angry, insulted or defensive.

Catch Yourself High-Leg

The first point in human change is awareness; you can't fix what you don't know is broken. Learn to catch yourself high-leg. What are your signs and symptoms? Do you tap your fingers or feet? Do you clench your jaw? Do you pace? Do you finish other peoples' sentences? Do you sigh? Become aware of your own body's signals that you're high-leg - then you can take steps to lower it and return to your calm, polite, empathetic, resourceful self. Following are two of the best strategies.

Positive Outcome Thinking (P.O.T.)

A way to change your mood and put yourself in a resourceful state of mind so you can do your best work.

Overview:

Positive Outcome Thinking (P.O.T.) means picturing things the way you want them to go. It means imagining a conversation going well before you have it. It means imagining a meeting being successful before you lead it.

How It Works:

Positive Outcome Thinking is by far the single most important element of success for any service provider, manager or executive. In fact, it is the most important success element for all human beings. It means deliberately focusing on the experience you want to have before doing a thing (visualization), then planning your actions and responses so as to increase the chances of success. P.O.T. is a planning tool.

The other thought habit - Negative Outcome Thinking (N.O.T.) means seeing things go wrong, and imagining how terrible that would be. N.O.T. leads to hesitation and F.E.A.R. (Fabricated Expectations Appearing Real). Anyone who has ever had to make a call to deliver bad news or discuss a touchy subject will be familiar with N.O.T. and how it makes the phone seem to weigh two-hundred pounds.

P.O.T. Step 1. See the event going the way you'd like it to go. See it and hear it in your mind. *"How would I like this to go? What do I want to experience? What do I want the other person/people to experience as we work through this event?"*

P.O.T. Step 2. Anticipate any likely problems or obstacles and make a plan to reduce/eliminate the possibility of them happening. *"What could go wrong? What questions might the customer ask? What objections might she have?"* *"How can I prevent these things from happening? If they do happen, how will I address them?"* Then devise remedies and solutions that will turn things back around.

P.O.T. Step 3. Once again, see the event going how you'd like it to go.

Tips For Managers:

Some managers are buffers of bad news and amplifiers of good news. They know instinctively that part of their job is to help employees make positive interpretations of the latest corporate developments from the executive team. These managers are encouraging P.O.T. Other managers don't take time to manage their own attitudes, so they pass their negative message on to their people by buffering the positive aspects and amplifying the negative. They encourage N.O.T. Reflect carefully on this question: Which type of communicator are you?

Adversity Questions

How to turn an adverse situation into an opportunity to perform at your very best.

Overview:

You can control your own attitude with precisely engineered questions. When faced with an adversity (a hassle, an inconvenience, an outburst, a setback, etc.), it is the questions you ask yourself that actually determine your emotional reaction. Ask yourself empowering questions (What's great about this? How can I prevent this in the future? What's the lesson here? What's another way to look at this?) instead of disempowering questions (Why me? How much worse is this probably going to get? What did I do to deserve this?).

How It Works:

So, the age-old advice is: Think positive. Refuse to allow problems and obstacles to dominate your mind. Catch yourself having negative patterns of thinking and immediately change those patterns to more positive ones. This classic advice is straightforward, and you'll get a thousand people in a room of a thousand to agree with it. But how? That's the part that usually eludes us. Over the years, I've found Adversity Questions to be the most powerful and yet the simplest way to instantly change your thinking and therefore take control of how you feel. The power of Adversity Questions lies in the power of all questions to instantly change your thinking process. When you ask yourself a question, your mind cannot help but try to answer it.

Adversity Questions:

"What can I control here?" (focuses you on what you can do, not what you can't do, prevents you from stressing over things you cannot control)

"Where's the opportunity here? How turn this around?" (helps you find options to fix/recover)

"What can I learn from this? How has it served me?" (helps you learn/ fail-forward/find meaning in failure)

"How can I make sure this doesn't happen again?" (prevention/ continuous improvement)

"What's another way to look at this?" (taps your creativity/innovation) "What's great about this?" (perspective/gratitude)

"What could be great? How can I make it great? (positive action/ recovery)

"What are my choices? What actions can I take? (positive action)

"Could I be overreacting a little?" (perspective, larger context)

These questions automatically cause you to shift your focus and perspective. Of course, some people will not adopt these new question habits because they see them as silly or impractical. There is another set of questions available to us which we tend to choose by default if we are unwilling to adopt the Adversity Questions.

Lousy Questions: *"Why me?" "What did I do to deserve this customer?" "How much worse is this problem probably going to get?" "How will I ever fix this?"* and *"How could they do this to me?"* If the Adversity Questions seem awkward to program into your mind as a new habit, consider the lousy alternative. The brain can't help but to answer any question you pose to it – so negative questions beget negative answers. Consider the quality of your day with negative questions like these running through your mind all day. They make bad situations worse. Think positive instead - and now you know exactly how.

Tips For Managers:

Adversity questions are equally powerful for managers to ask their employees any time they notice a negative attitude. Asking employees these questions makes it their idea and helps prevent the feeling of being lectured to. By creating a problem-solving atmosphere, the employee feels supported and the manager has just shown the employee how to approach a similar situation more effectively in the future.

Other ways to quickly lower your leg:

- **Take a walk to the water fountain.** Quick break to get blood flowing and change surroundings.

- **Take three slow, deep breaths.** Allow each exhale to calm you.

- **Take a 3-5-minute walk outside.** Fresh air and sunlight.

- **Have a small snack -** make sure you're not experiencing low blood sugar. Make sure you're not "hangry."

The 8 Hidden Concerns of Your Business Customers

Our next section is about making sure your customers feel good as you serve them. Have you ever encountered a customer who was just impossible to put at ease or satisfy? No matter what you did or said, you couldn't get them to relax and put their trust in you? You're not alone.

Of course, sometimes customers just don't like your answer (price, terms, delivery, policy, etc.) and nothing you do will satisfy them - if they can't have it, they remain upset. More often though, their lingering mistrust is caused by our failure to recognize an underlying psychological concern they have and address it on the spot.

Although the following eight concerns are related to one another, each one can be distinct to the customer and some may be more important than others. Any one of them – if not effectively managed – can affect the customer experience. As you examine the list, ask yourself two key questions: 1) Do I routinely look for these concerns in my customers so that I can manage them, or do I mainly focus on just the details and logistics of their issues? 2) Do I have any of these same concerns myself when I am the customer and I'm trying to get support from a supplier?

1. Concern about their own performance:

The customer may think, "If this goes wrong or if you cannot help me, it will negatively impact my job metrics. I'll look bad. My boss will be upset with me."

"You don't realize how badly this can affect me!"

If you sense this concern: Show empathy and understanding – say, "I can see there's a lot on the line here. I'll take care of you. I have a couple of options to help turn this around."

2. Concern about their own customer:

The customer may think, "I need your help to please my own customers. They are very demanding and I'm feeling the pressure."

"You don't realize the tight corner I'm in!"

If you sense this concern: Ask questions to understand...don't make assumptions. Then say, "I can see this is urgent and you need to take care of your customer. I have a couple of options for you..."

3. Concern about your understanding of their full situation:

The customer may think, "My situation is complicated; I need to feel certain that you have a full and complete picture of my situation and my needs."

"You don't have all the important details yet!"

If you sense this concern: Paraphrase. Ask, "So what you're saying is...is that right?" "I want to be sure I have all the details...you're saying ...have I got that right? Is there anything else I need to know?"

4. Concern about past bad experiences:

The customer may worry, "My last experience with your organization (or a competitor) was disappointing. I need to know it will be different this time."

"I'm afraid it will be like last time!"

If you sense this concern: Assure them by providing precise actions you and your team will take, timelines for deliverables and alternatives in case of unplanned circumstances.

5. Concern about your reliability.

The customer may think, "When you say you'll do a thing, I need to know I can trust you and rely on you."

"I need to know I can count on you!"

If you sense this concern: Show them your sense of urgency and responsiveness, but be careful not to overcommit. Manage the customer's expectations by explaining the steps you need to take and the process involved in serving them. Provide precise actions you'll take and timelines for completion.

6. Concern about your character.

The customer may think, "I need to know what kind of person you are. Are you engaged and committed? Do you love your job? Are you motivated? Are you good at your job?"

"I don't think you'll do your very best for me!"

If you sense this concern: Take ownership, brainstorm creative options for the customer, show your concern, paraphrase to show the customer your desire to understand. All of these actions will communicate your character to the customer.

7. Concern about your clout.

The customer may worry, "Am I speaking with the right person? Do you have the authority to handle my problem? If not, can you engage the right person?"

"I don't think you have the authority to solve my problem!"

If you sense this concern: Be aware of times when you'll need to involve your manager and assure them that you will. Clarify the steps you'll take to move the issue "up the food chain."

8. Concern about you withholding your best solution.

The customer may worry, "When you offer me options, I need to know they are the best possible options."

"I don't think you're making your best offer!"

If you sense this concern: Let them know what other options you have and explain the shortcomings of those solutions in order to better position the one you're offering. Specify how your offering will address each and every one of their needs.

Your Interpersonal Behaviors Make All the Difference

How to immediately gain the trust of your customers, suppliers and colleagues so they feel good like you do.

Some behaviors upset others, create one or more of the 8 Concerns and make them not like or trust you:

1. **Apathy** - *Not caring. Showing indifference.*

2. **Coldness** - *Refusing to show concern or compassion and instead coldly asking data questions. "Model number, please." "Invoice number, please." "I just need facts, please."*

3. **Brush-off** - *Trying to get rid of someone without finding help or directing them to help. "I can't help you." "That's not my department." "I don't know."*

4. **Rulebooking** - *Using policy as an excuse not to offer some kind of help. "That's our policy. There's nothing I can do."*

5. **Condescension** - *Talking down to others. Assuming they have no knowledge, expertise or experience. "Obviously it's because..." "Obviously you'll need to...of course."*

6. **Rigid Robotism** - *Making the customer follow your preferred procedure when none is required. Insisting on treating or interacting with every customer the same exact way.*

7. **Arguing** – *Bluntly and disrespectfully disagreeing. "You're wrong about that." "That's incorrect, no."*

8. *Self-justification* – *Defending yourself and absolving yourself of blame. "It wasn't me that created this policy." "That's not my fault."*

9. **Disappearing** – Not following up. Leaving the customer in the dark.

10. **Guessing** – Making up answers in order to avoid having to investigate.

11. **Not knowing** – Lacking knowledge customers feel you should possess (product/service knowledge, process knowledge).

12. **Acting completely powerless** – Acting like you have no authority whatsoever to handle the issue.

These are all high-leg behaviors. This is how we often act when we are failing to manage our moods. Take a moment and check the ones you sometimes do when you're high-leg. Result: No one likes you. Customers complain. Colleagues won't support you.

Some behaviors assure and affirm others, ease the 8 Concerns and make them like and trust you:

1. **Showing empathy, understanding and concern for their situation and their needs.** *"You're right, this is serious." "No wonder you called." "I can certainly understand why you'd want that." "I'm sorry you had to go through all that."*

2. **Showing warmth and friendliness** (but still some formality) as you interact with them.

3. **Taking ownership of the issue and seeing it through to the extent of your job function.** *"I'm going to do all I can to help." "I'm going to turn this around for you." "I'm going to put you in touch with someone who can help."*

4. **Being responsive and timely in your actions and communications.**

5. **Accuracy in your information, your projections and your promised next steps.**

6. **Demonstrating competence, knowledge, expertise.**

7. **Showing respect, consideration.** Allowing for the knowledge, expertise and experience of others.

8. **Showing a sense of urgency.** *"I can see this is urgent, here's what I'm going to do..." "I'll take immediate action to..."*

9. **Helpfulness** - a desire to do all you can to help.

10. **Offering viable options**. *"I'm going to develop some options and get back to you at x o'clock tomorrow." "I have a couple of options for you."*

11. **Being flexible, accommodating.**

12. **Following up.** *"I'm getting back to you like I said I would. Here's what I've done so far..."*

13. **Following through on your promises.**

14. **Providing frequent updates.**

15. **Showing cultural respect/sensitivity.**

These are all "balanced" behaviors. Your leg is down. Now we see the true importance of feeling good: You cannot build trust and create a positive impression on others unless you're feeling good. It's the only way to be at our best consistently.

Notice that all 27 of these interpersonal behaviors - the good and the bad - are all completely within your control. Nothing has to happen outside of you – no permissions, no conditions – before you can manage them. They are 100% up to you.

Forbidden Phrases

Phrases that offend customers or cause them concern - and how to replace them with the words customers like to hear.

Although we've talked about negative and positive interpersonal behaviors already, what follows are some all-too-common phrases that get used – in one form or another – by service professionals who are either oblivious or who have failed to notice their bad mood and how it's affecting their communication.

1. "I don't know." or, "That's not my job/department."

The problem: When you say you don't know, then stop talking, what you're really saying is "Please go away." Not a terribly warm message. Instead, try *"I don't know, but let me check."* or *"Let me go confirm."* or *"That's another department, but let me see if I can help."*

2. "You'll have to talk to x." or "You'll have to complete this form first."

The problem: It comes across like a command. No one likes to be given orders - especially customers. Instead try, *"Let's see if we can put you in touch with x."* or *"Why don't we complete this required form together right now. I've already filled in half of it for you."*

3. *"No." or "I/we can't."*

The problem: No one ever contacts you to be told what you can't do for them. They want to know what you can do for them. Avoid beginning a sentence with a negative. Instead try, *"What I can do is..."* or *"Yes, as soon as..."* For example, instead of saying, *"We can't send the onsite repair team until this form is completed,"* say, *"Yes, as soon as this form is completed, we'll schedule your visit with our onsite team."*

4. *"There's nothing I/we can do."*

The problem: Yes, there is. There's always something, however small, you can do to try and help. But even in those rare situations where there really seems to be nothing, try saying, *"I wish there was more we could do."*

5. *"That's not my fault." or "I didn't cause that problem."*

The problem: The customer doesn't care. Also, the customer now thinks your top priority is protecting yourself, not solving their issue. It may indeed not be your fault, but it's your responsibility to turn it around for your customer if possible. Instead try, *"Let's see if we can get to the bottom of this and work this out."*

6. *"I'll get back to you soon."*

The problem: It's too vague and it doesn't explain what you'll be doing while you're away. The customer may worry, and won't know how to update his own customer or manager. Instead *tell them exactly when you'll get back to them and tell them what you'll be doing while you're gone.* Just be careful not to overpromise. *"I'll go check with our inventory and shipping team and get back to you at 3:00 with an update."*

The Big Three - The Result of *Consistent* Interpersonal Excellence

If you could wish for three things you'd like your customers to think and say about you, what would they be? That you solved all their problems? That's not entirely up to you in many cases. That you delivered on the date they requested? That you succeeded in giving them the discount they wanted? Again, not always within your power. If you could have your customers think and say three things about you, it would have to be about things you can control. Try these on:

"I trust your competence and your character."

"I can see that you fully understand and can relate to my situation and my needs."

"It is clear to me that you are doing, and will continue to do, all you can to help."

Are these not the Holy Grail of personal commitment to customer service excellence? What an incredible accomplishment if you can conduct yourself in ways that make customers feel this way about you personally. You can - even if you can't always give them the specific things they ask for. In almost all cases if you are attentive, concerned, helpful and engaged; if you innovate options to help solve their problems; if you are patient and diplomatic; if you follow through and follow up - they will trust you and appreciate your efforts no matter what the final outcome. Why? Because they feel valued, respected, informed, assured, and trusting.

When you deeply apply the personal and interpersonal techniques we just covered in this section you will greatly increase the frequency that customers feel this way about you and how you managed their issue. You will enjoy your work more on a daily basis and find it more meaningful and rewarding as you look back on your day.

You may never hear these three things from your customers directly – we often only get a glimpse of a sliver of how they really feel about us – but that doesn't mean they don't feel your commitment and professionalism, and it doesn't mean they don't appreciate it. And you can sleep well at night knowing you gave your very best.

Competency 2 - Identifying the Requested Output and Receiving the Right Message
(clarifying context and needs).

Now that you are Feeling Good and you're doing all you can to help your customer feel good about the entire experience of working with you, it's time to get specific. The next part of your job is to get as complete a picture as possible of who the customer is, the context of their situation and what they need from you specifically. Any misunderstandings or assumptions at this point can lead to service problems down the road.

Have you ever gone off with good intentions but incomplete or inaccurate information and done the *wrong* thing *well* for your customer? Of course you have - everyone has. Getting this step right, however, allows you to do the right things right. Getting this step wrong means you may go off and do the wrong thing - with excellence. If you make assumptions about their details and requirements, this is easy to do. Key elements of this step include asking well-engineered questions, confirming existing and missing details and above all, avoiding assumptions.

Often when I ask my class for examples of things that can and do go wrong when serving the customer, they give me answers like, "Sending an invoice." What can go wrong when sending an invoice? Many things, it turns out: Wrong address, wrong discounts applied, tax mistakes, sent to the wrong person, wrong work done, referencing the wrong documents and double the quote. How many of these mistakes were preventable if people in the service chain had a way to avoid assumptions and notice incongruences? You need a tool that helps ensure you get what's missing, verify what's there and never pass on errors and omissions. That tool is called the Up-Front Checklist.

All human beings are vulnerable to cognitive biases - thinking errors. One of the most common cognitive biases that service professionals suffer is what I call **WYSIATI - What You See Is All There Is.** When you are busy (or perhaps even high-leg?) and you receive an order request document from a customer full of data, it's a common mistake to hurriedly look at it and assume that what you see is all there is - there's nothing more to know, nothing missing, nothing to check or add. As you know from experience, that's often not the case. You need a new bias that works for you rather than against you: **SIAM** (Something Is Always Missing). With this new bias, you take a skeptical view of any document with the intention to find the missing or inaccurate information you know from experience is likely there. Armed with this new, improved bias, the Up-Front Checklist will help you find what's missing.

The Up-Front Checklist

Get what's missing, verify what's there before you take action.

Thanks to SIAM, you'll be motivated to ask more questions and get the complete picture (or as complete a picture as possible at the time) before rushing off and engaging your network of suppliers and colleagues. The only way to ensure you consistently catch every important detail is to develop a checklist of things to verify up front, before you take action - and then make it standard work – normal operations.

Although the type of information you need to verify will vary depending on your business, your products and your services, these examples may help to illustrate the importance of a standard, evolving checklist:

- Is this the correct person to communicate with? Does she or he have the authority to make this request?

- Is their contact information correct? Is it the same as their shipping address, or is there a different address for shipping?

- Are all required documents completed - and completed accurately?

- Is their credit status up-to-date?

- Are there insurance issues? Are there warranty issues?

- Are there any other actions you'll need them to take that could cause a delay?

- Are there any regulatory or compliance issues?

- Do they expect to provision parts, or do they expect us to?

- What customer category or tier are they in?

- Have they spoken to anyone else about this issue? What stage are we at with them regarding this service issue?

Getting any of this information wrong can lead to serious service mistakes - mistakes that are totally preventable.

Sample "Context Report" for Escalating to A VP

Sometimes you'll need to escalate a customer problem to a VP. That VP will need a complete picture of the customer and the context in order to make a good decision. In order to provide as full a context as possible, reflect on the following questions and answer each one as accurately as you can. You may not be able to answer every question, but every bit helps.

1. Who is the customer?

2. Who owns them? Who heads up the company?

3. Where are they located?

4. What are their top priorities as a business (big picture/long-term)?

5. What are their top priorities as a business (small scale/short-term)?

6. What are the main interests of the owner/management team (big picture/long-term)?

7. What are the main interests of the owner/management team (small scale/short-term)?

8. What are their top concerns (big picture/long-term)?

9. What are their top concerns (small scale/short-term)?

10. In what service program are they currently enrolled?

11. What is the nature of the event? Do we have clarity on liability? What does each scenario suggest as a path: A) Likely our fault—keep them happy as we will pay anyway, B) Likely customer's fault—keep them happy as later a bill will come.

12. What's their overall mood with our company from recent history of our product performance and service excellence?

13. What are our goals with this customer in the short term?

14. What long-term goals do we have for this customer?

15. If any, what important political issues exist?

16. What significant financial issues exist?

17. What can we do for them, that they have asked for?

18. What can we offer them, that they haven't asked for?

19. For each potential offering, which departments will be affected?

20. What are the key company metrics that may be affected?

21. How will the decision affect each metric?

22. In light of all this context, what is your recommendation?

A lot of questions, right? How can we avoid annoying our customers with all these questions? With the Question Bridge.

The Question Bridge

Build a bridge of comfort and trust with your customer before you ask them an important question, then "walk" your question across the bridge - to them.

"Why do you ask?" "Where are you going with this?" "What are you going to do with this information?" "How does it benefit me to answer all your questions?" Anyone who has ever tried to ask a customer a series of important questions will be familiar with these kinds of spoken and unspoken reactions. They indicate mistrust and annoyance on the part of the customer. Many customer service professionals rightly worry about causing "question fatigue" when they have to follow a checklist of questions, even though it's in the best interest of

serving the customer well. In addition, some questions are inherently uncomfortable for the customer: *"What caused the damage?" "Have you paid your latest invoice?"*

An exchange in need of a Question Bridge:

Employee: *"Have you paid the last invoice we sent?"*

Customer: *"Why do you ask?!"*

Employee: *"I just want to be sure there aren't any inconvenient delays to delivery due to an outstanding bill. I know that would be frustrating."*

Instead, what if you rephrased your question to state why you're asking before you ask? It might look like this:

"Mr. Customer, in order to prevent any inconvenient delays to shipping, can I ask you to confirm that the latest invoice has been settled?"

Now the customer knows why you're asking, and they perceive a personal benefit in answering the question. You built a bridge of trust and comfort between you and the customer, then you walked your question across the bridge, where they more willingly received it.

Here are a few more examples:

"I want to be sure we don't overlook any discounts you're entitled to - can I ask you to provide your account number?"

"I don't want either of us to suffer any consequences of violating export regulations...can I ask you to confirm your country of operation?"

"In order to ensure we do the right fix and get you operating again as quickly as possible, it will help our technicians if they know in advance what may have caused the damage..."

"I sometimes find it helps my colleagues to set priorities if I can share with them what's causing the urgency..."

Be sure to state a positive benefit for the customer in your Question Bridge. It wouldn't be persuasive to say, *"In order to ensure I don't get in trouble with my supervisor, can I please ask you to confirm payment?"* There is no benefit to the customer in this statement so of course it has no power. In fact, it's even more annoying than asking the direct question.

Set up your Up-Front Checklist with a Question Bridge

It may have occurred to by now that you can also use a Question Bridge with your Up-Front Checklist. It might go like this:

"Mr. Customer, I have a few things I'd like to verify with you just to be sure we don't make any mistakes that cause delays - we want to get you your service just as quick as we can. It usually takes just a few minutes." Or,

"Ms. Customer, in order to reduce the chance of any preventable delays, I find it helps to verify a few details up front. Would that be okay?"

When you open like this, the customer now understands your reasons for wanting to go through your checklist with her and she sees a benefit in doing so. In short, you've sold the value of having the conversation with her. She's now motivated to participate in your process.

Verify Urgency

The next step to enhance your competency at identifying the need and receiving the right message is to the verify urgency when a customer expresses an urgent requirement. Certainly, there are often urgent requirements from customers and part of your job is to act with a sense of urgency and do all you can to rush your process for them. On the other hand, some customers automatically call everything urgent because of habit, or because they have learned it's the only way to get what they consider to be timely support. If you don't verify the nature of the urgency you may end up putting unnecessary stress on your supplier network. As a result, three things can happen: 1) You harm your own company because they assign resources to your issue while often putting other customers on the backburner, 2) You develop a reputation of always having your hair on fire and eventually your network stops believing you, and 3) You teach your customer that calling everything urgent gets faster results.

Always verify the urgency. Use a Question Bridge to do this without irritating the customer. Instead of asking, *"Is this really urgent,"* say, *"I understand there is urgency. I often find it helps my colleagues to set priorities if I can share with them what's causing the urgency."* Then be silent. The customer will more than likely feel compelled to share more details - then you can either offer options for the customer or indeed put valid pressure on your suppliers.

We'll cover this topic more in a future chapter when we talk about putting the right amount of pressure on your suppliers and colleagues.

Paraphrase to Confirm your Understanding

The final step in this competency is to be sure you understand everything correctly and to catch any miscommunications that may have occurred during the process. **Paraphrasing - briefly summarizing what the customer has said, to ensure complete understanding - is the single most important technique in this entire book.** It is one of the simplest skills to master and it provides the most benefit for the least effort. Consider its many benefits:

- It shows them you want to understand.

- It helps you actually understand better.

- It helps to calm them down if they are upset.

- In many cases it helps *them* to clarify what they actually want from you in the first place, because they don't always know.

Instead of *telling* the customer you understand (because maybe you only *think* you do), *ask* if you understand:

Instead of *"I understand,"* say, *"So what you're telling me is...and we need to...do I understand?"*

Instead of *"Got it,"* say, *"I want to be sure I've heard everything correctly. You're saying...and we need to provide you with...have I got that right?"*

Often the customer will add more detail or correct a misunderstanding - and this is the time to do it - *before* you take action.

Should you always paraphrase? Almost always. If the customer says, "I need a replacement part," you wouldn't paraphrase at this point and say, "Let me see if I've got this right. You're saying you need a replacement part?" This of course would be ridiculous. Paraphrasing means giving a brief summary, so in order for it to make sense, more information has to have been shared. Here is a simple way to remember: Paraphrase, don't parrot.

Competency 3 - Sending the Right Message (managing expectations).

Let's review where we are at this point in our Customer F.I.R.S.T. process: Competency 1 - **F**eel Good and help your customers feel good as a result of the interpersonal excellence you demonstrate because YOU feel good. Competency 2 - **I**dentify the need or opportunity and **R**eceive the right message by asking well-engineered questions to get the full picture and context, so you do the right things right instead of doing the wrong things right.

Now you need to **S**end the right message by making highly reliable commitments, educating customers to align their expectations with reality, deliver potentially unpleasant news where appropriate and handle upset customers when they occur. Doing each of these things right deepens trust.

Let's begin with making commitments to customers. Rule #1: Always make some kind of commitment. It could be to go look into the issue and get back to them, or to have the issue resolved during the call. Rule #1 is important because it prevents you from saying annoying things customers don't want to hear, like, "I can't promise you that." Well, what CAN you promise? Rule #2: Only make commitments you know you can keep. This is the key one. Have you ever told a customer you'd do something by a certain time, but you weren't sure? Did you cross your fingers and hope it would all work out? How did it in fact work out? Hope is not a business strategy. Never give a customer a promised based on hope; give them a promise based on the current reality ay the moment. If the current reality is that you don't know and you have to go talk to a colleague, then that's the commitment you make. Over time, the customer will learn to trust you, because they know you always do what you said you'd do.

The S.I.P.O.C. Commitment-Maker

A mental checklist for determining what to say when a customer makes a request—ensuring your promises are always kept.

Overview:

The S.I.P.O.C. Commitment Maker is standard work for determining how to respond to a customer request. It's easier (and more profitable in the long-term) to keep commitments that have been made accurately in the first place. The S.I.P.O.C. Commitment Maker is an adaptation of S.I.P.O.C. as found in Six Sigma improvement tools and techniques.

How It Works:

Let's assume for a moment that everything you do in your job that has value is an output. Outputs always have Customers, who require the Output from you, for which you follow a Process, which requires certain Inputs you get from your network of Suppliers. These five elements of your deliverables form the acronym S.I.P.O.C.

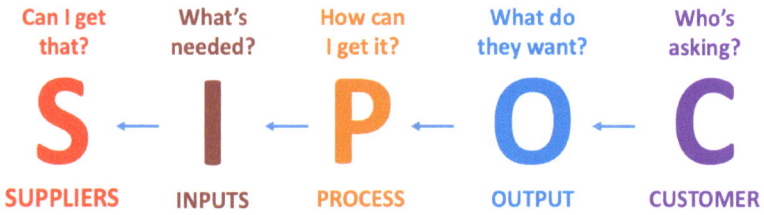

Can I get that?	What's needed?	How can I get it?	What do they want?	Who's asking?
S ←	**I** ←	**P** ←	**O** ←	**C**
SUPPLIERS	INPUTS	PROCESS	OUTPUT	CUSTOMER

To help you keep your commitments to your internal and external customers, you can use the S.I.P.O.C. model to run a "confidence check" before you make the promise requested by the customer. Working backwards, mentally move through each of the 5 elements of the deliverable:

Customer - Am I confident I know who's asking?
√I have sufficient experience working with this customer to be able to judge their circumstances and their needs.

√I possess a sufficient understanding of the contract requirements pertaining to this customer.

√I am confident that the individual I am communicating with is capable of sufficiently representing the needs of their organization.

Output - Am I confident I know exactly what they need?
√I have obtained the basic details of the request and confirmed that it pertains to my work function.

√I have followed a checklist of data to confirm with the customer to ensure complete understanding of their request.

√I have checked with the customer to confirm my understanding.

Process - Am I confident there is a process, and that I own it or influence it sufficiently to speak on its behalf?

√There is a clear, standard process in place to make / deliver the requested output.

√There is typically no significant variance in the output of the process.

√I own, control or influence the process sufficiently to predict and /or to control any variance in the output.

Inputs - Am I confident I know exactly what inputs will be required for the process?

√I know what materials and items are needed for the process.

√I know the scheduling and the quantities of materials and items needed for the process.

√I know where to obtain the materials and items required for the process.

Suppliers - Am I confident at this moment (because I'm being asked at this moment) that my suppliers can deliver the outputs in the timeframe required for the process to create the output for my customer?

√I know who the suppliers are, and I am confident they can deliver according to the input requirements.

√I have sufficient experience with each relevant supplier to judge their capacity at this time.

√There is typically no significant variation in the supplier output relative to this input request.

Virtually any problem within a value stream that relates to a missed deadline can be identified within the context of S.I.P.O.C.; perhaps you made a judgment error in clarifying who the customer is, or in exactly what they want by when, or in your process to deliver it, or in identifying the inputs you need for our process, or in determining that your suppliers could give you the inputs you need, when you need them. The most common trouble spots among the five elements of S.I.P.O.C. are the S and the I - determining whether or not the Suppliers can provide the Inputs needed within the timeframe you'd like to offer the customer.

If indeed you are confident in each and every S.I.P.O.C. element, go ahead and say Yes to your customer. If on the other hand you are not confident on one or more of the elements, give your customer a Can-Sandwich (which we'll learn about next) and go take action on whichever element had you concerned (ex. check capacity with your suppliers).

Here are some more examples:

"Let me go check with my team and get back to you in 30min."

In the above example, you were confident until you hit Process. It's not your process, or the process is too variable.

"Let me go check with inventory and scheduling and get back to you in 30min."

In the example above, you lost confidence at Supplier. You know who the suppliers are (since it's a process you are confident in), but you don't know at this moment if they can get you the inputs you need, in the quantities you need or of the quality you need, in order to meet the customer's specific request.

Again, two rules: Always make some kind of commitment, and only one you know you can keep.

One Promise You Can Always Keep

There is a promise you can and should make to your customers even when you have no idea what the outcome will be or how long it will take. This promise doesn't depend on anyone else, it is entirely within your control. It shows your customer that you are engaged and motivated to help them. It builds trust:

"I'll get to work on this right away and get back to you at X o'clock with an update on my progress."

Notice that it doesn't say, *"I'll get back to you at X o'clock with an answer."* You can't be sure when you'll have an answer - and at the same time, you can't say *"I'll get back to you when I have something."* That's too open-ended. It leaves the customer wondering if you'll be a day, a week, or if you'll get back to them at all. What happens if X o'clock rolls around and you still haven't got an answer or a solution for them? You call them back anyway, like you said you would. Instead of saying, *"I don't have anything for you yet,"* you say, *"I'm calling you back like I said I would. Here's what I've done so far...my next step is..."*

Tips For Managers:

Managers can encourage the use of S.I.P.O.C. by starting with themselves: When your executive boss makes a request, first run a mental S.I.P.O.C. to be sure that whatever commitment you make is one you can keep - and keep without damaging other aspects of the company. From there it follows that when your employees use S.I.P.O.C. to respond to your requests, allow them time to go and check capacity before making a commitment to you. If you don't do these two things, you're just absorbing pressure from above and passing it on to people below, all the while creating a string of hope-based commitments that have a high risk of failure.

Managing Expectations

Expectations are the experiences and results the customer anticipates as they do business with you. They can include expectations for prices, quality, turnaround times, delivery times, even communication and interpersonal style. Expectations can be high, low, positive, negative, realistic or unrealistic (compared to your current capacity).

Expectations are not always the same as needs. A customer may need a part delivered by the end of the week, but they expect you to be able to send it by tomorrow because you've done it before. A customer may not need a better price, but they expect a discount because they believe they are entitled to one. Because expectations are not always the same as needs, it is perfectly acceptable (and we would argue, essential) to *manage* them when they are unrealistic. If you are an orthodontist and your customer expects their teeth to be straightened within 6 months, but the process will actually take 24 months, you'll need to manage their expectations, or they'll never be happy with your service. And that requires education. No matter what else you do, you will never make a customer happy when they have unrealistic expectations.

So - when someone makes a request and you know full well the answer is No (for some regulatory-, process- or capacity-related reason), what is the best-in-class way to say it, in order to still show responsiveness and helpfulness? How can you manage expectations and still provide a positive customer experience? With the Can-Sandwich. Instead of telling them No, start with what you can/will do, then explain what you can't do and why - then immediately repeat (in the same words as the first time) what you can/will do. Let's take a closer look.

The Can-Sandwich

Manage expectations with education while still showing responsiveness and helpfulness.

1. Start on a positive, action-oriented note by stating what you can and will do for the customer. ***"What I can do is..." "I'm going to..." "Why don't I go ahead and..." "Here are some options - we can A or we can B..."*** No one in the history of business has ever contacted a supplier because they want to know what you can't do for them. So why start there? Why make that the first thing you say?

2. Make your limitations clear early on in the dialogue. Set clear expectations. That's easier to do now that you started off

on a positive note. *"I can't X..."*

3. Educate your customer so they understand the reasons for the limitation - this makes it a little easier for the customer to swallow. *"...because..."*

4. Immediately after step 3, repeat your commitment to the customer a second time. Tell them what you can/will do. You end on the same positive note on which you started. You say what you can do twice as many times as what you can't... ***"But again, what I can do is A or B...how would you like to proceed?"***

The Can-Sandwich

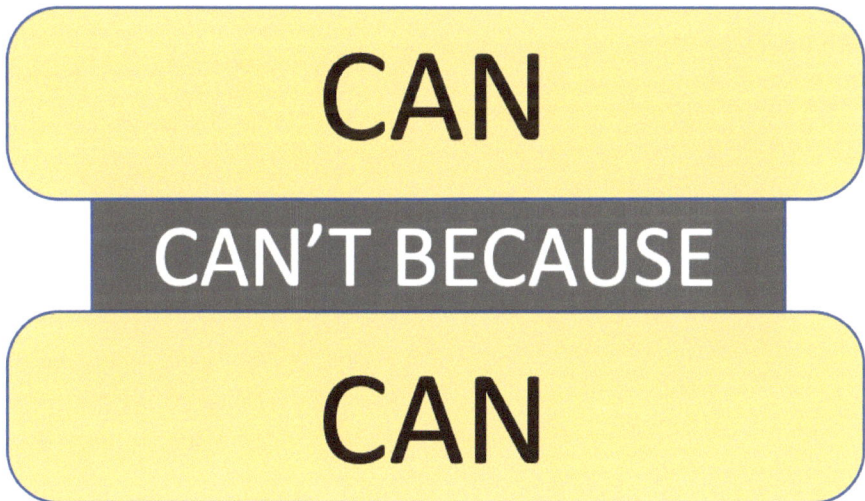

CAN

CAN'T BECAUSE

CAN

Customer: *"I expected it to take no more than 6 months to straighten my teeth. I really don't want to wait."*

Orthodontist: *"I can recommend a great dentist who can give you instant veneers, but you'll lose your original teeth, or I can begin right away with your treatment and have your original teeth straight within 24 months. It can't be done faster because we have to move the back ones first to make room. Plus, if we exceed maximum torque you could suffer broken teeth. But like I said, I can refer you to a dentist or get started right away with our natural process. How would you like to proceed?"*

The "Options" Can-Sandwich

Notice in the previous example that the orthodontist offered options to the client. *"We can A or B. We can't...because...but again, we can A or B - how would you like to proceed?"* This is a very powerful approach because it combines all the psychological power of the Can-Sandwich with the added power of choice. Customers want options to choose from. When only one solution is offered, they often feel trapped and powerless. If you can offer options, they feel that you are being more engaged and helpful.

Emphasize the Option You Want Them to Choose

Also in that example, did you notice that the orthodontist emphasized the option that he wanted the customer to choose? Research shows that in most cases when presented with options, customers automatically put more weight on the one that's emphasized, rather than make the effort to analyze for themselves.

"Would you like the red marker that's harder to see from a distance, or this black marker that's easier to see?"

"Would you like the omelette, the fruit plate, or our special congee breakfast, which is delicious?"

"Would you like a daily status report or is a weekly one okay, so you have fewer messages to have to go through?"

In each of these examples, unless the customer already has a firm idea of what she wants, she will tend to go with the one you emphasized, and the one you offered last.

How to Deliver Potentially Unpleasant News

Another important part of Competency 3 - Send the Right Message - is how you frame potentially unpleasant news. This is a big one, since every customer service professional has had to do it at one time or another - and some have to do it daily.

Warranty doesn't apply? Delay in delivery? It's going to cost more? Check didn't clear? There are some best- and worst-practices to keep in mind when conveying your message to customers effectively. But what does "effectively" mean?

✓ You don't accidentally *encourage* them to be upset.

✓ You don't make it *worse* than it has to be.

✓ You don't *increase* their worry, you ease it.

✓ You show them your good character and high competence, so they relax just a little.

✓ You *reduce* the odds they'll go over your head.

✓ You don't accidentally offend them with *blunt language*.

✓ You don't *overcommit* and make things even worse later.

When potentially unpleasant news must be given to the

customer, there are at least eight keys to keep in mind that will help to increase the chances the customer will hear your news in the best possible light and will allow you to maintain their trust.

1. Contact them promptly. Don't put it off. What's worse than getting bad news? Getting it late, or not at all. When you contact them promptly, you're showing them they're a priority to you. If you find yourself putting off the call, do P.O.T. (Positive Outcome Thinking) and plan the call so you feel more confident.

2. Contact them live. When you talk to the customer in real time – whether phone, video conference, or F2F – you can control their reaction and answer questions on the spot. It helps to prevent escalation and it shows them that you know how important the situation is. It also shows them you care enough to deliver it live. When you use email - even though it may seem more efficient - anything can happen.

3. Take action first, then report it. When you can describe the action you've already just taken to help turn around their issue, it shows your competence and sense of urgency; you ease their minds a little and cultivate more assurance and trust. If you haven't taken any action for the customer when you deliver your news, you have given them one more thing to wonder or worry about.

4. State your message neutrally. Avoid putting a negative slant on your message. Don't decide for them that your news is bad. instead, *state your message neutrally and let them decide.* The exception to this would be if you are contacting them for a second or third time on the same issue and you have unfavorable news to report regarding it. Avoid beginning with

"I have some bad news," or *"Unfortunately."* Some service providers are so certain their message is bad news that they actually help to make it a bad experience for their customer. They state their message negatively, then pause and wait for the customer to get upset. Then they try to manage the inevitable anger (which they helped to create). This is probably a mistake; it may be far better to try to take control of the dialogue with the customer and try to avoid any negative exchange where possible.

5. Frame it as an Update. Say something like, *"I have an update for you on x."* This sets a neutral tone and avoids pre-conditioning the customer to see it as bad news. They still may see it as bad news of course, but not because you have conditioned them to.

6. Use diplomatic language. Be careful not to use language that makes the customer's pain worse unnecessarily. Words like "declined," "rejected," or "cost" are unnecessarily harsh. However, being too indirect and diplomatic can seem evasive and dishonest to some customers.

7. Beware of the temptation to overcommit. Under pressure, it's tempting to overcommit – but doing so will only lead to more severe problems and erosion of trust later.

8. Try to finish your update with a choice of actions/options. Offering options, however small they may be, shares power with the customer and distracts them from complaining further as they shift their focus to choose one of your options. Instead of feeling trapped in a corner, your options offer them a choice of doors to get out and move forward.

Poor:

"I've got some bad news. Your replacement unit is going to be later than I promised. A part for the unit just got shipped in, and it's the wrong part. That means I'll have to re-order, and it's going to take that same seven days again so there's no point lying to you and saying it will be delivered on time, because it won't."

Better:

"Mr. Customer...(identify yourself)...I have an update on your replacement unit – I just had to re-order a required part. When we received the original order, it was the incorrect part, so as I said, we immediately re-ordered the part and it's rushing to us as we speak. Our new delivery target for your unit is now (state date), which is seven additional days, and I wanted to let you know just as soon as I found out. We are tracking the part as it is rushed to us. Would you like daily updates, or can we let you know once it has arrived?"

Poor:

"Your unit was declined for warranty. Because it was rejected, you'll have to buy a unit. A new unit is going to cost you $5,000. Please advise how to proceed."

Better:

"Mr. Customer...(identify yourself)...I have an update for you on your warranty request for the repair of your (item). In this particular case, warranty does not apply due to (specifics), but I have gone ahead and looked into some options for you...(share options)...how would you like to proceed?"

Handling Angry, Complaining Customers

If you're one of the few customer service professionals who haven't yet dealt with an upset customer, you will. Interactions with angry customers are among the most important conversations you'll ever have. They are an opportunity; they represent a turning point in the relationship. Handle it right and you'll be trusted for years to come. Years. Handle it poorly and the relationship will turn the other way.

Psychology of Complaints

1. A valid complaint is a gift. When customers believe (rightly or wrongly) that there has been a mistake or that they have been mistreated, this is valuable market feedback. The customer may be giving you important improvement data for your company. One verbal or written complaint is estimated to represent at least 20 other customers who did not make the time or effort to complain - and of course it is your duty to make things right - whether or not they have been harsh or rude in how they have expressed themselves. It always costs the customer something to complain. Have you ever told a restaurant server that everything was "fine" when in fact it wasn't? Why did you do that? Because you couldn't be bothered to complain. You knew instinctively that giving that "gift" costs you time, energy and risk, and that it may end up being all for nothing. When a customer complains, don't focus on what it's costing you; focus on what it's costing them.

2. Feelings are facts. When a customer is upset, many service providers focus on the facts and try to ignore the emotions. This is a mistake. There are many facts you need to handle and one of those facts is the way the customer is feeling. Feelings are facts. Acknowledge them. Respect them. Deal with them.

Don't judge then, ignore them, marginalize them or manipulate them.

3. You cannot reason with angry people. When human beings are angry their IQ temporarily drops several points. Our ability to think rationally is compromised. Angry people exaggerate; they want everything, free, yesterday. You must have them calm down first, then help them with their problem.

4. To avoid defensiveness in yourself, see their anger as a cry for help. In order to serve the customer well, you need to manage your own perspective. If you decide their angry behavior means they are rude, overbearing, disrespectful human beings you will become offended. If you decide their angry behavior is a cry for help; a good person having a bad day, then your attitude will become one of concern and helpfulness.

5. Get the sequence right: Step 1) Manage the person. Step 2) Manage their issue.

6. To determine if someone is upset, pay attention to the content of the message, not just the tone. Depending on the individual and their culture, they may or may not sound loud or angry to you. Some cultures are more low-key and polite, while others are more outspoken and passionate. A customer may be very upset yet sound as if they are calm; a customer may sound loud and vocal, yet not be upset at all. The one thing that you can always rely on to gage their anger is the nature of the message. Have they been mistreated? Neglected? Has a serious mistake been made?

Four Types of Angry Customers (Jagdip Singh, "A Typology of Consumer Dissatisfaction Response Styles," Journal of Retailing

66 (1990): 57-99)

Voicers. Voicers complain directly to the organization. If their complaint is resolved to their satisfaction, they will continue to do business, or continue with positive expectations. Voicers are in fact the best kind of unhappy customer you could hope for. The next three become increasingly worse.

Passives. Passives do not complain to anyone in your organization about a poor service experience, so you'll never get the chance to hear from them and solve their problem. They will eventually stop doing business with your company, if possible. And they will complain to at least 10 others.

Irates. Irates complain to your company, like Voicers, and they also complain to everyone else who will listen. They will spread the word to more than 20 people about how they were "wronged" and will boycott the organization. *They also leverage social media to spread the negative story.*

Activists. Activists are the ultimate unhappy customer. They take their complaint to higher authorities, such as lawyers, the media and the Better Business Bureau. They build websites, form coalitions and launch class action lawsuits.

Some customers start out as Voicers. Then as they are brushed off from one department to another and told no one can help them, they evolve (or devolve?) into Irates or even full-blown Activists. It is clearly critical that we handle angry customers with special care. The H.E.A.T. Model is a powerful psychological process that enables you to do just that - with consistent success.

The H.E.A.T. Model for Upset Customers

How to calm angry customers down and move them into productive problem-solving mode.

MOUNT IRATE

H - Hear them out.

- Use the Active Listening process. Listen for feelings as well as facts.

- Be sure to paraphrase. Say, *"So what you're telling me is,"* or *"Let me see if I've got this right..."*

- "I understand you received ACPC parts and you ordered ACM parts, is that correct?"

- "Let me see if I understand. You paid the bill on July 2nd and your last statement did not reflect that?"

- "So, what you're saying is that the repairs we made on your electric starter generator were supposed to be under warranty and we invoiced you for the work. Do I understand?"

E - Empathize and state your intention to help.

- Say, *"I can see this is serious,"* or *"No wonder you called,"* or *"You have every right to be upset..." "It is very easy to see why you need this resolved."*

- Encourage them to vent completely and at the same time, try not to get into concessions while they're still upset.

- State your intent to help and ask permission to ask some questions. Say, *"I'm going to do everything I can to turn this around for you. To do that, I need to ask some questions. Can I do that?"* If they're done being angry they'll say Yes. If not, do more listening.

A - Ask detailed questions (if required).

- *"Am I correct in thinking you'd like (an action to be taken)?"*

- *"Can you please confirm your shipping address/model number?"*

T - Take action to rectify the problem (if required and if possible).

- *"Here's how we can proceed - step by step..."*

Examples of Do's and Don'ts

Customer: *"You can't seem to do anything right! This is the third time you sent me the wrong part!"*

Don't: Defend yourself, make excuses, or pass the buck.

"It's not me who takes care of sending the parts."

"I told them the right part, they must have got it wrong."

"I didn't have anything to do with the other two times."

Do: Take ownership and signal your commitment to helping.

"I'd be upset too if I was sent the wrong part. I'll do what I can to help..."

"I'm sorry to hear that. Let's see if I can help turn this around for you."

Don't: Argue with them or make them wrong.

"I think we do some things right."

"Are you sure it's the wrong part? My records show we sent the correct part."

"That's because you didn't use the proper online ordering form."

Do: Acknowledge their point and then share your perspective.

"I'm checking our records as we speak...that's strange, our records show we sent the part number that you ordered. But of course you know best if it's the right part or not. I'd better go see what happened."

Don't: Be cold or indifferent.

"What's the part number?"

"I understand. What's the part number."

"Hold on a second." (then you go searching for the file or record).

"These things happen - we send out more than 200 parts each day. What's the part number?"

Do: Show warmth and concern.

"You have every right to be upset if you didn't receive the right part..."

"That's definitely not good. No wonder you called..."

"Well, I'm certainly going to help any way I can - can I ask you for the part number so I can bring up the file?"

Helpful Quotes:

"Don't talk people out of their anger; talk them through it." - Sam Horn

"When a customer is complaining, don't try and get them to stop; try and get them to finish." - Brent Finnamore

"It is often better not to see an insult than to avenge it." - Seneca

"First feel with them, then act for them." - George Eliot

"It takes less time to do the right thing than to explain why it was done wrong." - H. Longfellow

"The test of a first-rate intelligence is the ability to hold two opposed ideas in the mind at the same time." - F. Scott Fitzgerald

"It is one of the most beautiful compensations in life that no one can sincerely try to help another without helping themselves." - Ralph Waldo Emerson

Competency 4: Taking the Right Actions (Developing Reliable Solutions)

Now you and your customer are **F**eeling **G**ood, you've **I**dentified the need or opportunity and **R**eceived the right message and you've **S**ent the right message. It's time to focus on your supplier/colleague network and **T**ake the right action. There are a number of skills that can help make this process reliable and predictable.

- Using clear, precise language when you make requests and when you offer commitments.

- Creating a sense of urgency with colleagues and suppliers, but only when the urgency is valid and only in sustainable ways.

- Building *reliable* plans of action with gates and dates.

- Working differently with unreliable suppliers and colleagues to increase service levels.

- Developing Plan-B's in case of problems.

- Building & maintaining relationships as you do these things.

- Framing your requests to align with the needs, interests, metrics and priorities of others.

- Overcoming objections and resistance in a way that genuinely changes their minds.

First, Check Your Pressure

Before you run off and try to get your network to act with urgency, verify that urgency is genuinely real and needed. In a previous chapter we talked about the importance of verifying urgency before putting pressure on your network. Again, if you don't verify the nature of the urgency you may end up putting unnecessary stress on your supplier-colleague network. As a result, three things can happen: 1) You harm your own company because they assign resources to your issue while often putting other customers on the backburner, 2) You develop a reputation of always having your hair on fire and eventually your network stops believing you, and 3) You teach your customer that calling everything urgent gets faster results.

Your perception of urgency is informed by one or more of the following factors:

1. What the customer is asking for/expects. Not a valid source of urgency by itself. As we said before, just because the customer uses the word urgent doesn't necessarily make it so. Always verify urgency.

2. The method or style of the request – how they ask (angry, coercive, threatening, etc.). Never a valid source of urgency, but very tempting. When a customer raises their voice it's easy to assume greater urgency, but it actually has nothing to do with the actual details of the customer's situation. Again, always verify urgency.

3. Your own degree of stress at the time. Never a valid source of urgency. If you're high-leg and unaware of it, you can easily allow your stress to put an urgency spin on everything you do. Lower your leg and verify any urgency.

4. Your own automatic, unconscious habit of volunteering to rush most requests. Never a valid source of urgency. I've conducted role plays in my classes for years and without exception, I'll catch someone volunteering to expedite an order because it's all they know and they do it all day long. Learn to catch yourself offering to rush things unnecessarily.

5. The contract terms and conditions. Often a valid source of urgency, if terms and conditions promise fast turnaround times and delivery guarantees. But other times, you can leverage the trust you've built with them over time and find other, less urgent options.

6. Who is asking (position in your organization or the customer's organization). Often a valid source of urgency, if the requester is your VP, for example.

7. The actual, verified business need of the customer's organization that is driving the request. The true degree of urgency and importance. Always a valid source of urgency. This is determined by saying to the customer, *"I often find it helps my colleagues set priorities when I can share with them what's driving the urgency..."*

As you can see from these seven sources of urgency, only three of them are valid on their own (and only one of them is always valid – the other two are circumstantial and malleable). Based on this list, ask yourself how often you put pressure on your network unnecessarily. Before you apply the following skills to support the competency of Taking the Right Action, make sure you're not going into each situation with unjustified urgency.

Speech Acts – Language Tools for Making & Keeping Commitments

(Adapted from work by Chalmers Brothers, Language (2004): An accessible guide to using speech acts in the workplace and elsewhere. John R. Searle, Expression and Meaning: Studies in the Theory of Speech Acts (2008): Scholarly, seminal essays

representing 40 years of insight. J. L. Austin, How To Do Things With Words, 1962).

The fundamental unit of production in all organizations is the business discussion that takes place between colleagues. Business conversations are the starting point of all success and all failure. Organizations can have anywhere from 1000 to 100,000 business conversations taking place daily in the form of meetings, calls, emails, video conferences and written notes. Psychologists have wondered for decades about the key elements of an effective business conversation, and their research has shown that there are in fact four distinct parts to such conversations: Requesting, Offering, Declining and Accepting. If any one of these elements is done incorrectly, the conversation will result in failure. If they are all done correctly, the result is a clear, precise action or a highly reliable commitment to act.

Sometimes our words are themselves action; they make something productive happen that benefits the customer and the business. They are acts of speech that improve commitment integrity by codifying and making more effective the requests and agreements employees make with each other – which are at the core of all business discussions. Many of the Customer F.I.R.S.T. tools are based on the psychology of these four Speech Acts. An organization can only be productive if the business discussions everyone has consistently lead to explicit, time-based action. Misunderstandings and missteps are reduced; broken promises are diminished. Organizations become much more dependable in the eyes of their customers.

A Commitment is an explicit result promised to another, which includes 1) the specifics of the deliverable (quality, quantity, function) and 2) the precise timeline for delivery. A

Commitment involves five elements: Suppliers, Inputs, Process, Output and Customer. A commitment, by definition, means that the S.I.P.O.C. Commitment-Making process has been followed. Vague commitments ("I'll get right to work on this." "I need this ASAP.") are a problem because they cause mistakes, misunderstandings, expediting and customer dissatisfaction.

The 4 Basic Speech Acts

1. Requesting. Requesting is the act of explicitly asking a supplier for an action or a commitment. There are two applications of Requesting: Making a Request, and Accepting/declining a Request. Tips:

- Lower your leg.

- Verify any urgency before passing it on to your supplier.

- Make sure you're seeking the truth, not "What you want to hear."

- Tell the story; explain the need, impact, the context, and what's at stake.

- Know and respect lead times whenever possible.

- Make your request as soon as you know – don't wait (this shortens your supplier's window).

- Be precise – clarify what you need and set a deadline (propose a deadline for the sake of having one, if a real one is not necessary).

- Make it safe for them to decline and counter-offer something more reliable if they judge the need to do so.

- If you do not feel confident in the reliability of your supplier's commitment, use the T.E.A.M.S. model (explained in the next section) to set gates and dates and build highly confident options.

- Preserve the relationship – be respectful.

- Follow up.

2. Offering. Offering is the act of explicitly offering a deliverable, an action, or commitment to a colleague or a customer. Two applications of Offering: Making an Offer, and Accepting/declining an Offer. Tips:

- Offer a commitment, but only a commitment you can keep. Use the S.I.P.O.C. Commitment-Maker.

- Be sure you have accurate information before you offer help. Use the Up-Front Checklist.

- If necessary, offer to get back to them after having researched options.

- Make sure your offer approximates what has been requested and is not too far off.

- If appropriate, offer options – but only highly confident ones.

- If appropriate, provide updates. Don't disappear.

- Follow through.

3. Declining. The act of declining an offer or a request. Usually begins the process of negotiation, and is followed by another Offer. Tips:

- If you judge you cannot meet the Request, you must decline and make a counteroffer. Use the Can-Sandwich to show responsiveness and helpfulness.

- Manage expectations – educate the Customer as to why you cannot meet the exact Request.

- Use the S.I.P.O.C. Commitment-Maker to guide your response and decide whether or not to decline the Request.

- Refer to the tips for Offering.

4. Accepting. The act of accepting an Offer or a Request. Usually concludes the negotiation and results in an Agreement. Tips:

- The act of Accepting means you are both highly confident in the plan of action you have created together.

- Accepting an agreement or a plan of action is a mutual act; you are mutually accountable for the outcome.

All 4 Speech Acts should almost always lead to negotiation, in order to find a correct and sustainable balance between the "customer" request and the "supplier's" capacity – assuring the integrity of the Commitment. The supplier being Requested to make a Commitment considers S.I.P.O.C. before accepting a request.

Vague:
"I'll get right at it." "I'll get that for you as soon as I can." "Can you get that for me ASAP?" "Please do that as soon as you can."

Explicit:

"I'll have that for you no later than 5pm." "I'll have that for you at 3pm." "Can you provide that for me by 10am tomorrow?" "Please do that no later than noon, if you can."

With explicit phrasing the supplier now stands behind a clear commitment that wasn't there before. While this is a significant improvement in communication, such direct language can also create problems with relationships if spoken too abruptly or bluntly. Therefore, be sure to be explicit but also soft...

Direct, but hard:
"What is your commitment to me?" "What's your first critical step?"

Direct, but softer:
"Can I ask what your commitment to our customer will be?"
"Can I ask what your first critical step will be so that I can set a follow-up with you?"

The T.E.A.M.S. Model

A process involving Speech Acts to work with your suppliers and colleagues to build a set of highly reliable options to offer your customer.

Overview:
T.E.A.M.S. is a process you can use to work with your suppliers/colleagues to build a plan of action—*and commitment to that plan of action*— that is based on current capacity and has the highest possible chance of being delivered to the

customer with accuracy and timeliness. At its heart is the practice of gating the deliverable with check-in's.

Highly reliable options are ones that have a very high (80%) chance of success - you do what you said you'd do, when you said you'd do it. This is not always easy to do in a medium to large organization. J. D. Power said, *"The likelihood that a promise to a customer will be kept is inversely proportional to the number of people involved in making it happen."* Furthermore, some suppliers are more reliable than others. Some are in broken jobs that lack resources and support, some departments are too insulated from the customer, some individuals are disengaged, and some are simply incapable. The T.E.A.M.S. process is all the more important in such instances.

How It Works:

Once you understand the customer's issues and you've explained your solution or given them a Can-Sandwich, the next step is to engage your suppliers/colleagues, build a realistic plan of action and get their commitment to do their specific parts by specific times so that you can go back to the customer with a more reliable promise of what will get done by when. For many companies, that requires a major culture shift. It requires new and better conversations taking place between service providers and supplier-colleagues. In particular, it means getting clear explicit commitments from supplier-colleagues; commitments based on current capacity, not on best-case scenarios.

To accomplish this we begin with a dramatic shift in the mindset of the service provider as he or she communicates with the supplier. If you are a service professional, you already know what kind of shift I'm referring to: Remaining calm and easing up on the pressure placed on suppliers to "rush it," "expedite it," and "just make it happen." *If you are truly committed to making reliable promises to your customers, that means obtaining reliable promises from your suppliers, not ones that tell you what you want to hear.* Ask yourself this simple question: Do I want to build a plan with my supplier that is based mostly on hope or mostly on realistic confidence? The T.E.A.M.S. method will not work for you until you come to grips with the idea of building a highly reliable plan of action vs. getting your supplier to tell you what you want to hear. Once you are ready to hear the truth from your supplier, you are ready to work with him or her in a truly collaborative manner and create a highly reliable plan of action - one that may well fall below the customer's stated requirements. And we'll deal with that shortly.

The T.E.A.M.S. Model:

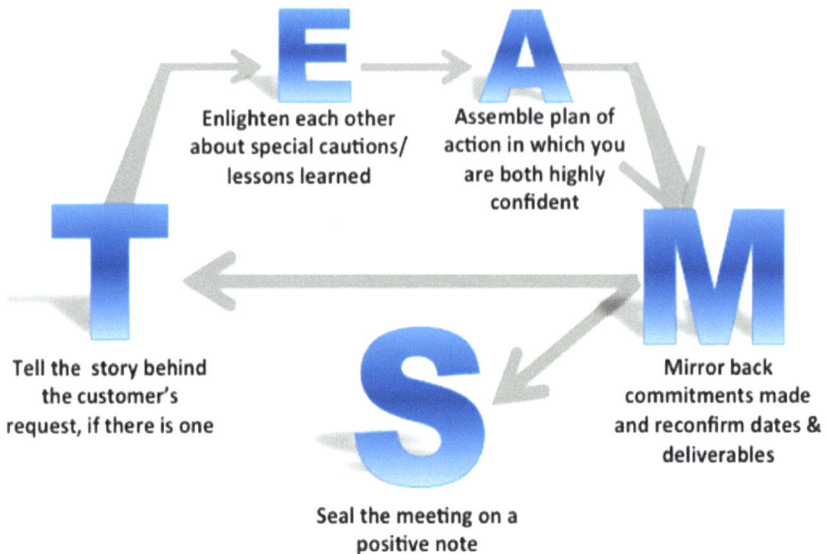

E — Enlighten each other about special cautions/ lessons learned

A — Assemble plan of action in which you are both highly confident

M — Mirror back commitments made and reconfirm dates & deliverables

S — Seal the meeting on a positive note

T — Tell the story behind the customer's request, if there is one

Tell - Tell your supplier the story/details about the customer's situation in order to provide context and establish importance. *"Here's what's going on..." "Here is the issue we need to think about...and here's why it matters..."* Use a question bridge with your customer to get the story. Then tell it to your suppliers.

Enlighten - Enlighten each other with any past experience and wisdom regarding the customer or the issue that should be kept in mind while assembling the plan of action. *"Anyone know anything about this? Anyone have any experience around this?"*

Assemble - Assemble a plan of action - with gates, dates and contingencies.

"What commitment can we make for our customer?"

"In case they ask, by when can we have that done?"

"Just to be sure we can deliver to our customer, what's our confidence level on a scale of 1-10 that we can have it done by then, and not later?" (looking for 8/10)

Special additional questions for less reliable suppliers:

"So we can update our customer, what's your first critical step, where things can sometimes take a turn?"

"By when would you say you will be able to have that first step completed?"

"What's your confidence level that you can have that step done by that time?" (looking for 8/10)

From here, several things can happen. They may convince you they can deliver, or they may raise doubts in your mind.

Explore those doubts. You may need to push out the number of days required for the first gate in the process. If so, ask how that might affect the end date and readjust if necessary.

If you sense your supplier is overconfident, ask, *"Is there anything that could come up and jeopardize that? What about X?"* or *"Can I ask what makes you that confident?"*

"If so, what's our plan B to stay on date? What kind of plan B can we make?"

American football coach Vince Lombardi said, *"Hope is not a strategy."* As you assemble your plan of action, keep the 80% confidence rule in mind: **Never go to a customer with a plan of action in which you are less than 80% confident.** Even then, an 80% confident plan is still relying on 20% hope. Even a 90% confident plan is still relying on 10% hope. Offering options to customers in which you and your supplier are 80-90% confident helps to ensure you can keep your commitment. Pressing your suppliers for best-case-scenarios and other forms of unlikely outcomes that are hope-based and require luck, ensures you won't likely be keeping your commitment. But you will be telling your customer what they want to hear in the short term.

As you assemble your plan, you may need to have options ready in case the customer isn't satisfied with your plan. First, where possible, build a plan of action that gives the customer what they want, when they want it. If this cannot be done with high confidence, resist the urge to coax your supplier into a shaky commitment and instead, build two more options:

1) Offer the customer what they wanted, but not when they wanted it.

2) Offer the customer an alternative, for when they wanted it, or very close.

But remember, these options still have to be highly confident, or you simply don't offer them. That's the tricky part, because many service reps focus on the price, terms or delivery date they'll need to tell the customer. They are focusing on the wrong number. The only number that matters is >80%. That means whatever the plan and its options, both you and your colleague are 80% or more confident they will be realized.

Here is a question we get asked by one or two impatient participants every time we workshop this method with our client groups: *"Where's the option to try and improve the dates? When can I try to better the dates with my supplier and push them to do better?"* My answer is this - once you've built your plans and options, you can revisit them and try to better them - but NOT at the expense of your mutual confidence level. You must begin with a solid, stable plan - you can't fire a cannon from a canoe. An 85% confident plan that's a few days later that the customer originally asked for is far superior to a plan that meets the requested date but is only 40% confident (and therefore is relying 60% on hope and luck). Focus on the most important number - the one that represents the truth. The flowchart on the following page illustrates this process.

Mirror - Mirror back a summary of agreements. *"So let's review...we have decided to do this...that...using this...being taken care of by...and I'll check in by...do we agree?"*

Seal - Seal or end the meeting on a note of confidence. *"Are we convinced we can do this? Does anyone want to involve their manager? We've got a great opportunity here, and a great plan."*

Your Customer Bill of Rights

As you work with your supplier to build a reliable plan of action, keep in mind your Bill of Rights - it provides for you the moral strength to push (in a friendly, respectable way) for accuracy and accountability:

1. You have a right to request a firm, clear commitment from your suppliers, and you have a right to be given one.

2. When commitments are broken, you have a right to ask for an explanation, and you have a right to be given one.

3. You have a right to help and support from your manager in getting these things.

```
                    ┌─────────────────────────┐
                    │   Highly Confident       │
                    │  Plan/Offering (s) (80%+) │
                    └─────────────────────────┘
                                │
                    Does it meet or come close
                       to customer's needs?
            ┌──────────┐
            Y          │
            ↓          N
    ┌───────────────┐
    │   Offer it     │
    └───────────────┘
                    ┌─────────────────────┐
                    │ Try to improve it so │
                    │ it does – but at NO  │
                    │ COST to confidence   │
                    │       level          │
                    └─────────────────────┘
         We were                  We were
         able to.                 not able to.
                    ┌──────────────────────────────────┐
                    │ Develop a set of highly confident │
                    │ (80%+) alternatives to offer      │
                    │ customer:                         │
                    │ Option 1: What, but not when      │
                    │ Option 2: When, but not what      │
                    └──────────────────────────────────┘
```

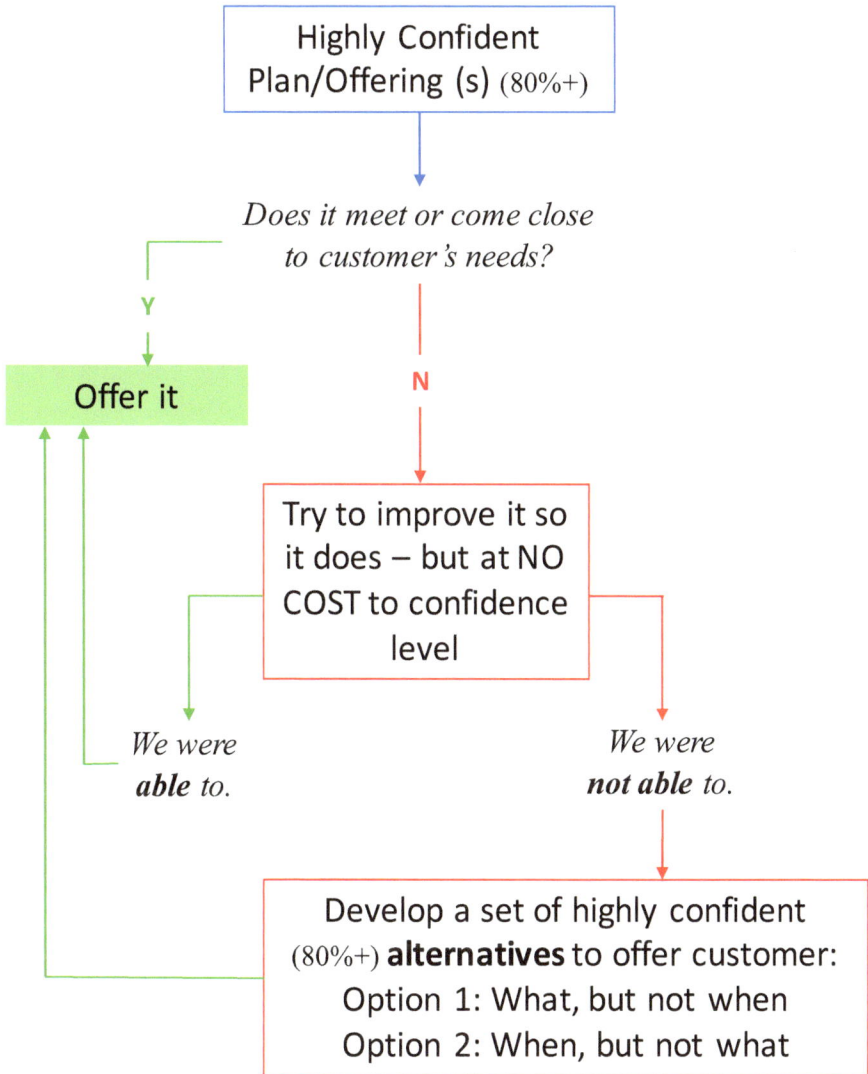

Asking vs. Telling

As you look back at the T.E.A.M.S. steps, notice a pattern - other than the Tell step, everything else is a series of questions. Questions have the effect of engaging the other person in the process. When you ask a question, the other person can give you their answer; but when you tell them something, they may disagree. This is where commitment comes in - involvement leads to commitment. No involvement, no commitment. One simple yet powerful way to involve suppliers in a plan of action is to ask them rather than tell them, so it's their idea and not yours. As an example, consider these possible approaches to requesting a deliverable from a colleague or supplier:

1. *"I need this done and shipped by May 12."* This isn't even a request; it's a command. While it is specific, which is good, it is dangerous; you run a risk of sounding bossy. Furthermore, you've made it all about you, not the customer.

2. *"My customer wants this shipped on May 12."* Your customer? How about our customer?

3. *"Our customer wants this shipped by May 12."* Better, but still a command and still no involvement opportunities for the supplier.

4. *"Our customer has asked to have it shipped by May 12, but I told him I'd need to talk to you first. Here's the story...so what kind of commitment do you think we can make for our customer?"* Now you're providing context, showing respect, and inviting them to problem-solve with you.

What to do if they still don't deliver

In the end, nothing works every time. There are too many variables in supply systems, even internal ones, for things to go smoothly all the time. In fact, the TEAMS system recognizes this inevitable fact – which is why you must schedule a check-in – set gates and dates with suppliers in order to catch snags as early as possible and try to find alternatives. As you have your

TEAMS conversation with your supplier/colleague, you create a plan that might look something like this:

Either mentally or on paper, you have assembled a plan of action including gates and dates with your supplier. It looks something like this:

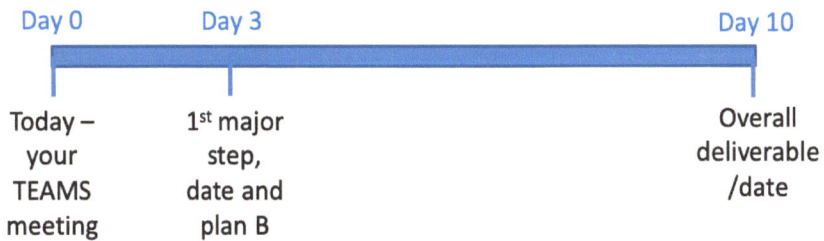

Day 0	Day 3		Day 10
Today – your TEAMS meeting	1st major step, date and plan B		Overall deliverable /date

According to this particular plan, they have committed confidently to have the deliverable within ten days and have also committed to have the first key step completed three days from now. What do you do if, on day three, they don't have the first step in their process completed and they didn't let you know – like they promised to?

As the following diagram illustrates, you need to have a conversation with your supplier/colleague. When I ask people in my classes what to do, they say the first thing to do is find out when they can get the deliverable. That is the wrong answer. You want to preserve the relationship, but you don't want to let them completely off the hook.

First ask what happened. This begins an important learning conversation. Next, talk about what can be done to prevent it from happening again and again in the future. Finally, talk about the current deliverable. And should the conversation end up with your supplier/colleague brushing you off and not providing reasonable answers, remember your Bill of Rights and press the point a little. Otherwise, you can be sure it will happen again.

Have a conversation about the missed deliverable.

1. *"What happened? Did we miscommunicate?"*
2. *"How do we prevent this from happening again? How can I help?"*
3. *"What do we do now to get back on track with this specific deliverable?"*

Tips For Managers:

For many employees the idea of seeking explicit commitments from their colleagues is daunting. They fear upsetting their colleagues or worse, raising complaints. Make sure your employees understand and trust that you will back them up and keep them safe as they apply this tool. You must have an "I've got your back" conversation. Then you have to mean it when it counts – even when it's inconvenient for you.

Influence and Persuasion Skills

By far, the most important aspect of anyone's job is to be able to mobilize others (suppliers, colleagues, customers, employees) and gain their active support. To perform your job well, you need suppliers and colleagues to get back to you promptly, give your issues a high priority and work with you to build highly reliable plans of action. You need your customers to provide timely feedback on requests and quotes, know and follow lead times for orders and deliveries and provide complete, accurate information when placing an order. Some people think it should not be necessary to influence others, since people *have to* perform their functions and the process requirements themselves should motivate everyone. But this view is simplistic. In today's organizations people are being continually asked to do more with less and resources are diminishing - all in an effort to maximize return-on-capital. As a result, people often feel overloaded, so they have to make judgments, and those with the most influence tend to receive the most support. In addition, many people in the work force have grown up questioning authority and position. They don't respond well to being told what to do. They need to be shown the logic and benefits of doing what you ask.

3 Sources of Influence:

Position Influence. In all organizations there is an unwritten rule that everyone should respect the position of the person making a request. And it's not just about hierarchy; even a CEO can be hesitant to veto safety recommendations from their safety officer. Your position as a manager gives you a degree of influence with your subordinates and with other managers. Your position as a customer service rep gives you a degree of influence regarding customer issues.

Relational Influence. Your success in building interdependent, reciprocal relationships and networks with others gives you a degree of influence. People with the right connections have more influence than people who go it alone. Also, becoming a member of a high-visibility coalition with an important mandate gives you influence.

Personal Influence. By far the most powerful source of influence, personal influence is what you have left when Position and Relational influence are peeled away. Personal Influence is the result of your knowledge, expertise, reputation, energy, self-confidence, relationship building skills and communication skills. This makes it possible to lead without authority and to influence people with whom you have no organizational clout. People want to support you not because of your position and not because of who you associate with, but because of who you are as a person and the talents and skills you possess. *As a general rule, individuals who are likable, trusted and who understand the needs of others tend to get served first and get served better.*

The Personal Influence skills that follow will enable you to achieve this like never before. You'll be able to gain agreement, get buy-in, change minds and overcome resistance more effectively so people *want to do what you want them to do*.

The term "influence" can have many meanings and many people have a negative view of influence because they confuse it with manipulation. For our purposes, let's have it mean this: **Personal Influence means using true facts and sustainable methods to affect the views, opinions and actions of others toward mutual benefit.** By this definition, influencing others is an ethical, positive thing. It builds trust, strengthens relationships and sparks collaboration. The world needs more of this kind of influence.

Manipulation, by contrast, means trying to affect the views, opinions and actions of others without relying on truth, using unsustainable methods (coercion, lies, guilt, bribes, threats) to benefit you alone with no regard for the impact on others. Common examples of manipulation include exaggerating your demands in a negotiation, concealing your true intentions, deliberately providing false information and threatening to go to a VP if your needs aren't met.

Influencing others requires four basic things:

1. A sound, logical argument. Of course, it helps to have a reasonable request or idea in the first place. And that request should not be seen to cause damage (interruption, increased costs) without justification.

2. Credibility/trust. The more people trust your character and your competence, the more credence they will give to your opinions and requests.

3. Effective communication skills. You have to be able to clearly explain yourself and clearly understand the views and responses of others. That includes reading between the lines and hearing things not said.

4. A thorough understanding of the other person's interests, needs and concerns. People do things for their own reasons, not yours. The better you know them – their needs, goals, concerns and pressures – the more effectively you can frame your request in a way that appeals to them and triggers their interest.

We will continually refer to these four things as we explore the skills that follow.

Throughout the course of your week, if you're like most B2B service professionals dealing with complex customer issues, you no doubt interact with dozens of different people as you do deal with shipping issues, product customization, repair planning, sales support, supplier management, and so on. Your network of such colleagues allows you to get things done for your customers. If you think about it, however, there are about 10-12 people that you *most* need to rely on, not dozens. Thinking about who those dozen people are and identifying them is one of the most important things you can ever do to improve your customer service performance.

Your Strategic List

A Key-Person list to focus your influence efforts.

Make a list of the 12 or so people you need to interact effectively with the most, in order to do your best work. Some of them will be people who depend on your outputs, while others will be people who you depend on for your work outputs. Start with the obvious: Your manager(s). Your teammates? Someone from shipping? Technical service? Legal? Engineering? Product development? Marketing? Sales? Field service? Customer training? Publications? Take some time and build your list thoughtfully. These are the people who you most depend on in your work. Your work affects them, and theirs, you. You have reciprocal relationships with these people. Communicating well with them and having good relationships is fundamental to your success, and to the success of your company.

For each person on your list, note your current level of influence with them (how well you get along, how easily you communicate, how much or how little resistance they give you, how reliable they are, etc.). Beside each name, write "OK," or "Improvement needed." Your goal will be to use the skills in this section of the book to maintain the OK's and to improve the others.

But there is another reason for creating and studying this list. High performers have higher quality individuals in their network. Your influence efforts will have more success when they are applied to people who are already action-oriented by nature. Sometimes a network develops by chance, other times people are assigned or suggested to you. Boldly seek out people who are:

- Reliable - they do what they say they'll do.

- Responsive and take initiative - they get back to you quickly and they have a bias toward action.

- Trustworthy - they speak the truth.

- Reciprocal - they understand the value of give and take.

- Creative - they readily innovate solutions and options.

Examine the people on your Strategic List with these criteria in mind. If any of your contacts seem to be lacking these traits, strongly consider finding replacements. This will be a process that takes some time, but remember - Personal Influence skills will not change who they are as people; you cannot change someone's personality traits.

Building Quality Relationships

Gradually develop mutual disclosure and deeper familiarity with your suppliers and colleagues as human beings, not as production units.

Next to flat-out getting things done, building quality relationships with the people in your Strategic List is the most important activity you can ever do. Showing a genuine interest in someone's children, karate, antique car or hiking passion creates a bond that engages them with you emotionally. Equally, sharing little bits and pieces of your own hobbies and passions builds rapport and gives you both a chance to connect as human beings from time to time - rather than being all business.

Benefits of Building Relationships with Customers and Colleagues

- They are more responsive and helpful.

- They give your requests more priority.

- They are more forgiving when you make a mistake.

- They give you more information and insight.

- You have a deeper understanding of each other's priorities and goals.

- There is more trust between you.

- You both enjoy working with each other more.

Who in the world wouldn't want more of these benefits? They make everything easier. And they give you more influence with each other.

Test Your Current Relationship-Building Progress. For each person on your Strategic list, see if you can name their passion hobby. Either write down their passion hobby - rock climbing, running, piano, photography, poetry, etc., or write DK (don't know). Then follow the same procedure for children - "3 kids," "no kids" or "DK". Next, write down each person's place of birth (city, not country). Finally, write down each person's "couple status" - "taken," "single" or "DK".

How did you do? You can see in an instant whether you do as much relationship building as you think you do. These are things you cannot help but get to know about others over time - even by accident - unless the two of you are all business all the time. Each DK is costing you the benefits we listed previously. Each DK is an opportunity. How much more trust and comfort would there be between you if you could say, *"Oh by the way, how are your horses doing with the cold weather we've been having?"* or *"By the way, how's Karen doing? As I recall, she started college this year?"* or *"Oh, I almost forgot - I found a great blog on marathon running and I thought you might like it."*

A participant in a Customer First class once shared an interesting story about a colleague from another facility with whom he struggled to get support on a regular basis. His colleague always replied late to his requests and consistently put up barriers which caused frustrating delays. One day during a phone call, he happened to reference his hobby of playing bass guitar. Immediately the colleague replied, "You play bass? Me too!" There was an instant energy and warming between the two of them as they discovered they had both played in bands, they both liked the same rock music, and they both admired many of the same bass-playing heroes. "Since that day," the participant shared, "He responds immediately to my requests and regularly goes the extra mile to support me." As you learn more about a colleague, you never know what kinds of hidden connections you may have - and you'll *never* know unless you engage in some degree of relationship-building activity.

Best Practices for Building Quality Relationships

- **Share a little about yourself here and there.** Sharing brief stories about your weekend or you vacation allows others to get to know you better and become aware of your humanity. Even if they don't share back, it still improves the relationship and creates familiarity that will be of benefit. Caution: Nothing controversial, nothing creepy. Until you get to know them well, they don't need to know about your membership to a controversial club or about the details of your recent attempt to remove a mole from your butt. Don't "overshare."

- **Share about yourself that which you'd like to know about the other person.** Want to know if they like sports? Tell a quick story about your favorite sport. Want to know if they have kids? Tell them what you did with your child last weekend. Sometimes it will prompt them to reciprocate with a similar story of their own - and now a door has opened.

- **Ask general, safe questions about their lives from time**

to time. Direct questions like *"Are you married?" or "Do you have children?"* are invasive. Instead, ask, *"How was your weekend?"* or *"Any plans for the holidays?"* or, *"How has the weather been where you are?"* Then the person can answer any way they wish, but it may lead to a good conversation and an opened door.

- **Look for open doors.** When someone opens a door, go in! When someone mentions their kids, their passion hobby or their latest vacation, all "safety" locks are removed - you can (and should) ask all the questions you want. They've opened the door on the subject and you are free to take an interest. In fact, not pursuing the subject for a minute or two is considered rude.

- **Look for commonalities.** You both have twins? You both enjoy cycling? You both like playing guitar? You both fundraise for the same cause? These shared interests are powerful emotional bonds. They make great conversation starters and create immediate and lasting rapport.

- **Do not drone on endlessly about yourself.** Sometimes an individual will think he's a people-person but in fact he's not; he is only interested in himself, telling endless stories about himself and never taking an interest in the lives of others. In fact, sometimes that individual is a Topper - she always seems to have a better story than yours. It makes others want to avoid her because she eats up their time and bores them. Not exactly a helpful habit.

- **Balance your needs with concern for others.** Sometimes you need something from a colleague so urgently that it can be tempting to ignore their concerns and push for it. But if you marginalize the concerns of others, you'll lose trust – even if you've already built rapport and found things in common. Instead, acknowledge their concerns and work with them to create alternatives. You might be inconvenienced now, but the long term payoff in trust will be a fruitful investment.

- **Be sensitive to privacy but don't be put off by it.** Some people are more reserved and private than others. This has nothing to do with you personally. If someone is reluctant to share or does not seem interested in your personal life, 1) Don't assume they are unfriendly. 2) Don't assume they don't like you. They are private, and that is neither good nor bad. At the same time, don't let this fact dissuade you from continuing to share little stories about yourself from time to time. It will still have a positive cumulative effect.

- **Understand and respect cultural differences.** In some cultures, it's normal to begin with business and end with a quick personal exchange. Other cultures do the exact opposite. In some cultures, friendships are few and deep; in others, people have many friendships, but they are more superficial. Remember: The goal is to cultivate a relationship that feels good to both of you.

Armed with these best practices, revisit your Strategic List and see who you need to improve relationships with. Set a goal to get to know each of them a little better over the next few months.

Remember: Your goal is not to turn them into best friends, the goal is to make some kind of meaningful connection – however small it may be.

Choosing the Right Communication Medium

There are three elements of our communication that have an impact on the receiver: Body language (facial expressions, hand gestures, posture, etc.), tone of voice (and other voice qualities such as volume, speed and intonation) and finally our actual words themselves. Research shows that not all elements of our communication have an equal degree of impact on the receiver.

How we read each other F2F
(impact, impression & likeability)

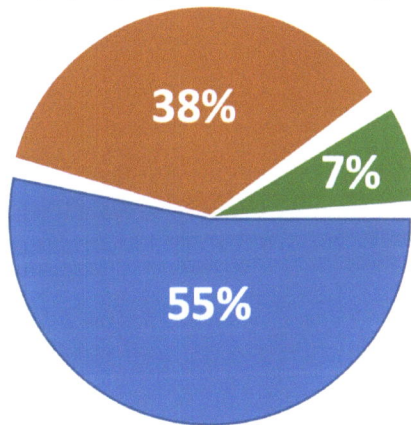

As the graph above shows, body language is responsible for more than half of the impact you have on others when you communicate. More than a third of your impact comes from your voice, and the actual words you choose have less than a 10% impact (Knapp, Hall, 1972; Scherer, 1972; Starkweather, 1961; Burns, Beier, 1973; Ekman, 1985; Mehrabian, 1975; Hall, 1969).

Recent research on video conferencing (F. Roberts, 2020. N. Bloom, 2020, E. Bernstein, 2020) shows us that even though we see each other's "faces" on video calls, our influence is reduced by 50% due to the imperfections of technology (latency, jitter, packet loss, and unnatural frames-per-second transmission). It just doesn't feel the same to either party.

Choose the Right Medium for your Task

Face-to-Face
100%
55% body language
38% paralanguage
7% actual words

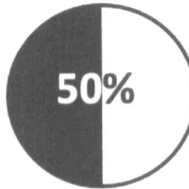

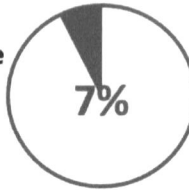

Video Conferencing
50%
18% body language
25% paralanguage
7% actual words

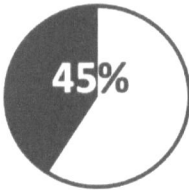

Non-WiFi Phone
45%
0% body language
38% paralanguage
7% actual words

Email/text
7%
0% body language
0% paralanguage
7% actual words/emojis

Knapp, Hall, 1972; Scherer, 1972; Starkweather, 1961; Burns, Beier, 1973; Ekman, 1985; Mehrabian, 1975; Hall, 1969; Haggard, Isaacs, 1967; Druckmann, 1982; Motley, Camden, 1988; Drummand, Hopper, 1993; Duncan, Fiske, 1979; Rosenfeld, 1984; DePaulo, 1980; Greene, 1985; Streeter, 1977; McCormack, Parks, 1990; Hale, Stiff, 1990; Kalbfleisch, 1992; Burgoon, 1990; Buller, 1991.

The takeaway: **To transmit data use email. To influence, use phone, video conferencing, or ideally F2F.** How many times have you tried to get someone to take an action using email and struggled to get them engaged? Now you have insight as to why - you were rendering yourself 93% ineffective.

The Four Quadrants of Human Intention (Personality Quadrants):

A guide to building instant rapport with others no matter how they are behaving or communicating.

Overview:

When human beings communicate with each other they have many different emotional and cognitive intents. As many intents as there are, they can probably be boiled down to four. We communicate with others to achieve one of four broad intents at a given time: Either to get attention, make a connection, get something done or to increase precision and clarity.

Rapport is defined as the reduction of differences. It means matching the intent of others; reducing our differences with others. It means speaking to them as they like to be spoken to, and making their intent yours. Rapport building is an essential skill for service providers because it is the foundation of influence, and service providers need to constantly be influencing customers and suppliers. How can you build rapport almost immediately with anyone? By understanding some basic characteristics of their current intent and the surface personality that temporarily emerges. The Personality Quadrants tool helps us not only gain a better understanding of our customers' and colleagues' communication intent, but also our own preferred intent too.

How It Works:

As powerful as relationship building is, you can do even more to connect with your customers and colleagues. As you take ownership of the customer's issue and try to resolve it, it's also powerful to build psychological rapport with the customer. Psychologists have demonstrated through research that establishing rapport as you communicate creates a marked increase in your effectiveness. Rapport means speaking to others as they like to be spoken to.

There are many psychometric instruments available to organizations that help us understand ourselves and others, but unfortunately many of them involve so many variables that it becomes difficult to quickly get the gist of another person without asking them what their "four letters" are. While the Personality Quadrants tool is general and lacks the detail of other instruments, it provides a superior means of quickly getting a sense of the other person's communication style and primary psychological intent. We refer to this as their surface personality. Notice HOW your customer is communicating – direct or indirect? Loud or soft? Then notice WHAT they are talking about – business issue or personal story? Formal style or relaxed style? Details of a task or trying to make a personal connection? Once you identify which quadrant they're in at this moment (we move around throughout each of the four quadrants during the day), adjust your communication style to match theirs and you'll be able to influence them like never before.

Of course, people are far more intricate and complex than these four boxes, and there is much more to each individual than the descriptions we're providing here. It's important to remember the limitations of this model as we focus on its strengths and uses.

Analyzing Andy is someone who's current intent is to *get things right*. When a customer or colleague is in this mode, he is indirect and task focused. He is emotionally controlled, diplomatic in communication, and somewhat reserved socially. He seeks details, values accuracy and precision and loves to problem solve. He is most comfortable following processes and procedures. He dislikes pressure and overly excited or overly flashy people, and he is somewhat risk adverse. When you are speaking with an Analyzing Andy, state your intent to be accurate and precise; avoid being too enthusiastic; use logic to support your proposed course of action; provide details and be open to discussing his concerns about contingency plans and risk mitigation.

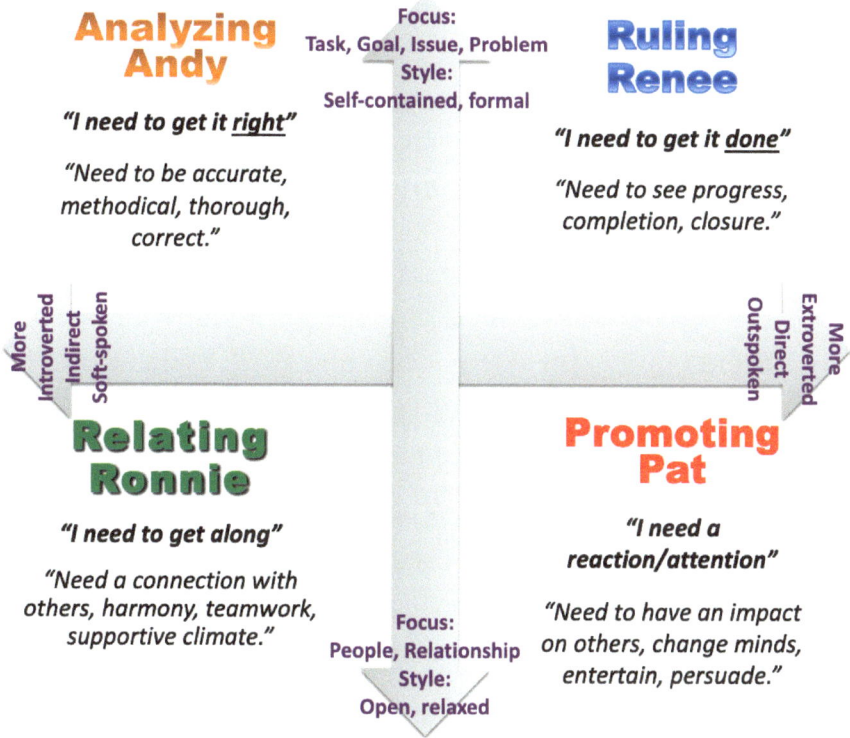

Analyzing Andy

Focus: Task, Goal, Issue, Problem
Style: Self-contained, formal

"I need to get it right"

"Need to be accurate, methodical, thorough, correct."

Ruling Renee

"I need to get it done"

"Need to see progress, completion, closure."

More Introverted Indirect Soft-spoken

More Extroverted Direct Outspoken

Relating Ronnie

"I need to get along"

"Need a connection with others, harmony, teamwork, supportive climate."

Promoting Pat

"I need a reaction/attention"

"Need to have an impact on others, change minds, entertain, persuade."

Focus: People, Relationship
Style: Open, relaxed

Ruling Renee is someone who's current intent is to *get things done*. When a customer or colleague is in this mode, she is direct and goal-focused. She is a decision maker and a natural leader. She communicates directly and even bluntly, because she finds it to be more efficient and allows her to control situations. She values bottom-line results, not empty promises. Delays and distractions annoy her. When you are speaking with a Ruling Renee, state your intent to be fast and efficient; to help her achieve the results she needs; take ownership of the issue;

be assertive and firm; focus on deliverables; keep stories and background data to a minimum; demonstrate the merits of your proposed plan of action and align it to her business goals.

Relating Ronnie is someone who's current intent is to *get along or make a connection*. When a customer or colleague is in this mode, he is indirect and relationship focused. He is indirect like Analyzing Andy, but for different reasons. He wants to avoid upsetting or hurting others. He is relationship focused and is very supportive and helpful to others. He prefers harmony and camaraderie in his network and dislikes confrontation and conflict. When you are speaking with a Relating Ronnie, state your intent to support him and his team; make a strong personal connection - meet warmth with warmth; avoid being too loud or intense; and above all, make it safe for him to express his concerns or to give bad news.

Promoting Pat is someone who's current intent is to *get attention or a reaction from you*. In this mode, she is direct and people focused. She tends to project energy, confidence and charisma. She is highly persuasive and very likable. She values attention and appreciation from others. She is highly persuasive. She is a dreamer and loves to imagine possibilities. She dislikes details, routine and structure. When you are speaking with a Promoting Pat, show energy and enthusiasm for her stories and jokes; show that you value her ideas and opinions; relate your ideas to her plans and interests; make her feel like a VIP; and never make her wrong or lose face.

Which Personality Type Are *You*?

Although we all tend to move around during the day from one intent to another, it's also true that we all tend to favor one or two intents over the others. When you think deeply about your own natural preferences and behaviors, you'll discover that you feel most comfortable, most like yourself when you are in one of the four intents (and for some people, possibly two of the intents equally). This is important for us to know about ourselves because our own primary intent can act as a perception filter for how we perceive others. For example, people in Ruler mode view Analyzers as slow, Relators as soft, and Promoters as distracting. People in Analyzer mode view Promoters as untrustworthy and Rulers as pushy.

Talk to others from their intent quadrant, not yours.

Of course, all of these tools and skills in the Persuasion component of F.I.R.S.T. are secondary to actually resolving the customer's issue. The most important overarching criterion for serving your customers is to correctly identify their needs, promise only what you know you can deliver to them and then follow through and deliver it with distinction. The benefit of the persuasion and influence tools and skills in this section of the book is that when you do all this, you can also make it a positive and pleasant experience, thereby standing out from your competition all the more. And if you cannot give the customer what they want, then using these tools and skills can help make it all go down easier - improving customer acceptance of your limitations and acceptance of your proposed alternatives.

The Difficult Person 3-Step:

How to break through difficult customer behavior and prevent it from happening again.

How It Works:

Whether a supplier, colleague-partner, or a customer, a difficult person is someone whose behavior is interfering with your job or making it hard for you to get your objectives accomplished. They may be blocking you with aggressive behavior, tying you up with endless questions or criticisms, ranting and raving or completely shutting down and not giving you what you need to do your work. Whatever the situation, difficult behavior is a serious problem that affects your work and often your personal happiness.

Before we explore coping techniques however, we need to differentiate them from average everyday unpleasant people: There are many different kinds of unpleasant people - those who don't like you, or who you don't like; those who disagree with you all the time, or those who just seem to push your buttons and rub you the wrong way - one might say the chemistry isn't good. These are not Difficult People as we're addressing here. The key to coping with unpleasant people is perhaps to refuse to let them upset you; practice stress management techniques of letting go and not giving people permission to upset you.

One important criterion to keep in mind in addition to "nuisance people" is whether or not they have the capacity to behave normally. A Difficult Person is someone who has the mental and emotional capacity to behave normally but is currently choosing not to. If you've ever seen someone bully one person but be respectful to their own boss, then you know. Yet there are many people in the global workplace who hold professional positions and are largely able to function despite having mental or emotional challenges that make it difficult for them to behave normally. One simple way to know is to apply the techniques that follow. If the person remains difficult, or they behave the same way in the future, there's a good chance they're not capable of behaving differently.

Assuming you are in fact dealing with a difficult person as I am defining it here, you are probably going to take an approach that falls into one of the following categories:

Fight - Do battle with the other person. Attempt to force them into change through the sheer force of your arguments. Whether it's done overtly, through negative confrontation, or covertly through sneak attacks and undermining, fighting ruins relationships and raises complaints. Not a good option.

Flight - Remove yourself from the battlefield: get yourself transferred to another department or another customer, or put someone else between you and them to act as a liaison. The flight option is expensive. It involves a lot of time and resource commitments. Not a good option.

Flow - Do nothing, but stop letting it bother you. Great for unpleasant people, but not for difficult people because you aren't solving the workflow interruption problem.

Fret - Do nothing, but continue to suffer misery. Too many people make this choice - simply because they believe they have no other choice. Misery is of course an option, but not a very attractive one.

Fix - Change your behavior in positive productive ways, thereby inspiring their behavior to automatically change. The difficult person is capable of behaving differently but for some reason is not. Because they can in fact behave better, there is hope. You can change your own behavior and instantly have an impact on theirs.

A formula that I've found consistently works well is what I call the 3-Step Formula. Difficult people are a fact of life. You cannot change difficult people. Fortunately though, you can get them to behave differently. How? By changing your own behavior. First, manage the person. Then, manage their issue. The Difficult Person 3-Step Formula is a tool for getting through to difficult customers or colleagues and connecting with them.

Step 1: See the intention, not just the behavior. What is their primary fear? Sometimes it is very difficult to see past the behavior.

Step 2: Give it to them. Ease their fear. Don't withhold what they need just because you don't like the way they are asking for it.

Step 3: In the future, ensure they always get it, so they don't revert back.

Difficult customers come in many forms, and the model that follows shows us four of the most common forms: Grizzlies, "Experts", Nothing people and Criticizers.

Difficult behavior flows from fear; when a customer fears their primary intent is in danger, they become difficult. The actual service issue is not a factor here - rather, it's the customer's perception about the situation and their fear of what might happen next.

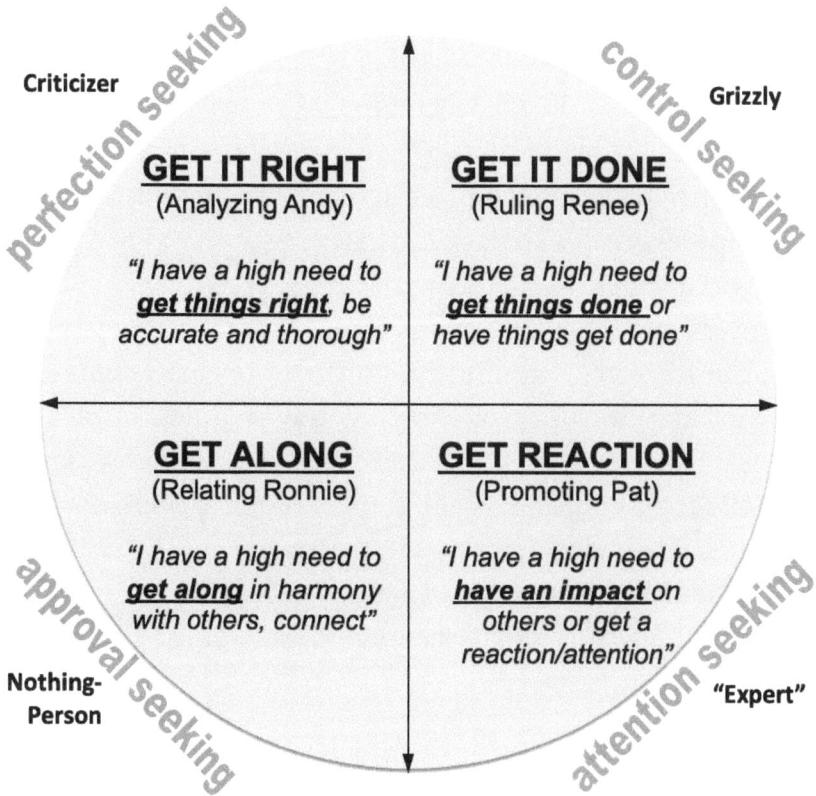

When Rulers fear things aren't going to get done, they become Grizzlies. When Analyzers fear things aren't going to be accurate, they become Criticizers. When Relaters fear there's going to be confrontation, they become Nothing People. And when Promoters fear they aren't getting enough attention they become "Experts". As you interact with them, give them what they want; give the "Expert" attention. Give the Grizzly assurances that you're in control. Give the Criticizer an open forum to express his concerns. Give the Nothing Person your assurance that you won't get upset with them.

How to transform customers with a high need for recognition and validation: Understanding "Experts"

Promoters want to get a reaction. When they feel this intent is being threatened, they may become an "Expert". Attention-seeking talkative people who are in "Expert" mode think they're right. Sometimes they are, and therefore they're not really a difficult person. But sometimes they're not right. They are self-proclaimed experts on whatever subject is at hand and their ego demands satisfaction. As customers, they perceive themselves to be special, and want to be treated as such. What do "Experts" fear? They're not going to get the attention, the treatment they feel they deserve, or they're going to be wrong and look bad. What do they need from you, that you can give them? Recognition, attention, appreciation, special treatment, respect for their customer status and extensive knowledge or experience. Agree where you can, and offer your perspective in a respectful tone, without making them wrong. Use phrases like:

"It's great to talk to someone who has experience in this area."

"You make a good point. At the same time though..."

"I can see why you'd think that. In fact, in our experience we've found that..."

"Based on your experience in these kinds of things I'm sure you already know that..."

How to transform customers who won't give feedback or share their thoughts: Understanding "Nothing" People

Relaters want to get along. When they feel this intent is being threatened, they may become a "Nothing" Person. A person who is in Nothing mode is very frustrating because they use silence as their device. They are so concerned about disappointing you or about creating a confrontation with their answers and issues, they feel like the only thing they can do is say nothing at all. No feedback, no comments, no answers - even if the issue is urgent. Or they may just say that everything is fine, when in fact it isn't. What do Nothing People fear? Upsetting you, creating confrontation or disappointment.

What do they need from you, that you can give them? A safe climate where they feel they can trust your reaction, an open dialogue based on mutual support and reassurance. Use phrases like:

"I really need your help..."

"Whatever you need to tell me, please know that it's okay..."

"I get a sense that you're not happy with my response. If you can tell me what's troubling you, I'd be very grateful..."

How to transform customers who are attacking you personally over a service issue: Understanding Grizzlies

Rulers want to get things done. When they feel this intent is being threatened, they may become a Grizzly. When someone is in Grizzly mode, they are highly confrontational, intense, loud, pointed and angry. They are pushy, outspoken and aggressive. Often insulting and offensive. They are the ultimate "In your face" person. What do Grizzlies fear? Things aren't getting done, deadlines and objectives aren't going to be met, productivity will be lost, the service provider is not in control of his or her own team and cannot make the right things happen. What do they need from you, that you can give them?" They need you to stand up and take ownership, to understand what's at stake and take charge of the situation like they would if they were you. Use phrases like:

"Here's my commitment to you..."

"Here's what I'm going to do..."

"I can see why you'd feel that way. Here's what I'm going to do to turn this around..."

How to transform customers whose extreme need for details are consuming your time: Understanding Criticizers

Analyzers want to get things right. When they feel this intent is being threatened, they may become a Criticizer. People in Criticizer mode have a standard of nothing less than perfection - and nothing ever meets it. Because they expect everything to be flawless and efficient, they are chronically seeing imperfections and problems. Their relentless search for accuracy causes them to pick apart and berate almost any view or opinion. They can always find something wrong in anything anyone says or does. Meetings drag on, discussions lose focus and momentum suffers. What do Criticizers fear? Things are falling apart, mistakes are being made or could be made, problems will arise. What do they need from you, that you can give them? They need to know that you care about accuracy and details, and they need to go over possible problems with your proposed solution. Use phrases like:

"I'm so glad you want to explore all possible scenarios. I feel the same way..."

"You make a good point. Let's discuss the details that concern you the most..."

"Here's our plan of action...of course, it's not perfect."

Try Hard Not to Judge

Perhaps the greatest challenge in dealing with difficult people is our own reaction to their behavior. When someone demands recognition or demands action in a rude way it can be difficult to "give them what they need" because we're so busy being offended by their words. We don't want to give them what they need because we feel they have no right to demand it in the first place. Yet it is exactly that attitude that will cause us to withhold what they need - and therefore we become part of the problem.

As you look back at each of the difficult person types, which one offends you the most? Which one flips your switch and makes you want to judge them for being unfair or unrealistic? That's probably the one you need to focus on. You need to examine your reasons for being of- fended, where other people just like you might not be, or not to the same degree. Do they remind you of someone else? Do they remind you of a part of yourself that you'd care not to recognize? Do they take you back to a difficult experience you suffered from your past? Whatever the case may be, it is important to find a way to relax your judgement so you are open to giving them what they need, authentically. Until you release your judgement of a difficult person, you will be unwilling and unable to transform their behavior.

The Greatest Influence Principle of All: People Do Things for *Their Reasons*, Not Yours

When it comes to influence and persuasion, there is no greater rule than this. Recall that one of the 4 things needed to be a good influencer is a solid understanding of the other party. Do you know how to make your ideas and requests interesting to the specific individual you're addressing? Do you effectively adapt your message to appeal to their interests? Do you support your ideas with reasons the other person finds compelling? There is no bigger mistake you can make when attempting to engage your suppliers and colleagues than to give them *your* reasons why they should help you. Equally ineffective is to give them a list of benefits and hope that one of them strikes their interest (a technique known as *feature-puking*).

Never try to get someone interested in your idea. Instead, you need to know what the individual's interests, goals and concerns already are, and then link your request to one of those. That way, you don't have to create new interest; you're appealing to an interest that already exists. The result is that they enjoy the process more (people like to talk about their interests, so suddenly you're no longer pestering them) and you don't get exhausted from trying to create something new.

P.O.T. Revisited

Recall that P.O.T. (Positive Outcome Thinking) is a planning and visualization tool you use to picture things going the way you want. Applying this principle (that people do things for their own reasons), we have another use for P.O.T.: Before you speak to someone to persuade them to take an action, invest a few minutes and think about what their concerns, goals, metrics, pressures and needs might be. If you already have a good relationship with them, this will be easier to do accurately. Then connect your proposal or request to one or more of those interests and goals. Now you are ready to approach them with your idea.

EXAMPLE 1 - **Johnny and his math studies.**

The situation: Johnny, your nephew, is 13 years old and struggling with math. He is at risk of failing. You need to persuade him to study more in order to get better grades.

His interests and concerns: Because you know him, you are aware that Johnny wants to be an astronaut more than anything. You also know that his greatest concern these days is having to repeat a grade.

Your goal: Convince Johnny to study more in math.

What would your specific behavioral request be for Johnny? How would you position your request so that it resonates with him and is compelling to him?

EXAMPLE 2 - **Mr. Phillips and his parts-ordering habits.**

The situation: Mr. Phillips is the procurement manager for your customer company, a fractional aircraft leasing firm. Phillips has a history of ordering parts from you at the last minute, leading to expediting and struggles with negotiating added costs. You are aware from past experience that he knows the lead times for parts orders, but he seems to ignore them.

His interests and concerns: Mr. Phillips's company has a goal to be known as "The fractional ownership company that always has a jet ready for you." His company's chief concern is decreasing the frequency of grounded aircraft.

Your goal: Convince him to order parts within published lead times.

What would your specific behavioral request be for Mr. Phillips? How would you position your request?

We'll revisit these two examples shortly.

The Pain/Payoff T-Chart

How to position your requests to appeal to the needs and interests of the other person.

The goal in persuasion is to get them to *want* to do what you want them to do. Show the other person how they can get what they want most and avoid what they want to avoid most by doing the thing you want them to do. When you can make the connection between getting what they want (payoff) and avoiding what they want to avoid (pain), you can persuade them effectively, position yourself as a trusted advisor and improve the relationship.

It is important to plan both the payoff message and the pain message. Some people are naturally more motivated to gain perceived payoff (peace of mind, prestige, security, favor, approval, etc.), while others are naturally more interested in avoiding perceived pain (rejection, mistakes, stress, financial strain, etc.). Imagine two people out for a walk or jog. One could be motivated to lose weight or avoid diabetes, while the other could be motivated to gain energy and youthfulness. By preparing to speak to both sides of human motivation, you'll be more likely to hit your persuasion target.

1. Identify the action/behavior you need the other person to do, or to do more often. Make sure its specific, observable and something you have a right to ask for. In the previous example with Johnny, it might be, *"You need to study math three times each week."* In our example with Mr. Phillips it might be, *"Order parts within our published lead times."*

2. Reflect on what their top interests/priorities/concerns are. If you don't know, you may need to start paying more attention to the hints and clues their conversations can provide. You may also need to ask. For example, *"Ms. Customer, so that I can keep your top priorities and concerns top-of-mind as we serve you, can I ask what some of your most important issues are in your business right now?"*

3. Connect your requested action/behavior to one of their highest priorities. *"If you (take this action), then that will give you (some relevant benefit) , which then leads to the (the big, target benefit) you want. And achieving B is a top priority of yours, isn't it."* Two keys here: 1) Create an irrefutable chain of logic, one than cannot be questioned or argued. 2) Cognitive ease - don't make it too long, with too many links in the chain.

4. Connect your requested action/behavior to one of the things they most want to avoid. *"If this action doesn't get taken, I'm concerned it might cause (a relevant problem), and that of course could affect (the deeper problem you know they want to avoid)...and that's the last thing we want to see happen, isn't it."*. Once again, remember to create an irrefutable chain of logic with cognitive ease.

Begin with your Payoff statement for Johnny: *"If you study your math three times each week, that can lead to better grades, right? And better grades make it possible to get into the right university, don't they. And as you know, getting into the right university is critical to being accepted into astronaut training."* Then deliver your Pain statement: *"At the same time, if you don't study harder in math there's a risk you could fail, right? And if that happens, you may have to repeat the year, and I know that's the last thing you want, isn't it."*

Your Payoff statement for Mr. Phillips: *"If you order parts within our published lead times, we'll be able to deliver on time more consistently so you can do your repairs on time - which supports your goal of always having a plane ready for your customers. And that's a key objective for you isn't it."* Then deliver your Pain statement: *"And if parts are not ordered with lead times, we run the risk of sometimes missing your deadline right? And that can lead to delayed repairs and grounded aircraft - and I know that's the last thing you want to see happen, isn't it."*

TIPS:

1. The order of operations is important when building your pain/payoff statement. (1) Clarify the behavior you want the other person to do. (2) Identify their top priorities, interests and concerns: What do they want? What do they want to avoid? (3) Build a connection between the behavior you want them to do and the priorities you know they care about.

2. Make sure to be respectful and not to offend them or appear to be threatening them with consequences. Instead, view it as an attempt to help protect them from negative

consequences you are worried about them experiencing by not taking action.

3. If it seems like you're just reminding the other person of things they already know, consider two things: a) If they knew, they'd be doing it. b) Everyone needs a top-of-mind reminder from time to time. Use phrases like *"As you know,"* to avoid appearing condescending and talking down to the other person.

4. Finish each statement you make with a confirmation that encourages them to agree, such as, *"..and that's something we both want, right?"* or, *"...and that's the last thing either of us want to see happen, isn't it."*

Sometimes your Pain/Payoff statement will cause the other person to suddenly become consciously aware of the logic of taking action. That's a very good thing. Often, however, your Pain/Payoff statement will draw out the other person's underlying objection that has been keeping them from action all along. That is also a very good thing...

Resistance Busters

How to transform resistance into acceptance, and objections into agreements.

As a service professional in the middle of a value chain or value stream, you want to be highly effective at persuading and negotiating with two primary groups of people: The people downstream (your customers) to have realistic expectations and to take certain actions that help you serve them better, and the people upstream (your suppliers/colleagues) to make realistic commitments and then to deliver on time. All experienced professionals, whether in customer service or sales know that the moment you attempt to persuade another person, you invite resistance. To overcome resistance, you need to have the right attitude toward it and see it as an ally, not an obstacle. Resistance is a normal, natural part of the persuasion process. To the average professional, resistance is something to fear. To the persuasion master however, it is welcomed because it is both expected ahead of time, and also understood to be a normal part of the process of changing someone's thinking.

Step 1: Anticipate objections and prepare counter arguments.

You may recall that one of the four things required for Personal Influence is a solid argument. So, we're back to P.O.T. again - Positive Outcome Thinking. Before you ever talk to your customer, supplier or colleague, anticipate their likely objections, concerns and questions. Then prepare your solid counterpoints. *"If they say this, I'll point out..."* *"If they say this, I'll remind them of..."* The self-confidence that comes with this kind of preparation alone is worth the investment of a few minutes. When you finally do deliver your Pain/Payoff statement and their real objection surfaces, you'll think to yourself, *"Great. Your objection is right on time and is exactly what I thought you'd say."*

Step 2: Always begin with agreement, then state your persuasive point of view.

Have you ever tried arguing with someone who keeps agreeing with you? Good luck. As powerful as agreement is, many people will actually agree with 95% of what a person says and still focus all their attention on the 5% they disagree with! No wonder they can't persuade anyone of their point. When you agree with someone, agree! Try not to state the exception to the rule or the one situation where it wouldn't be true. All that does is make them wrong and you lose rapport with them. When you don't agree, agree anyway. Find some aspect of truth in what the other person says or believes. When you can't agree on anything the other person expresses, you can at the very least agree with their right to feel like they do. When someone resists your attempts to influence or persuade them, agree. Always agree! Result? They lower their shields and become receptive to your message.

Agreement Examples:

"The Earth is flat." *"I agree it sure looks flat, and maps of the world are always flat. On the other hand, circumnavigation has shown that the Earth is actually round."*

"Cats are exactly the same as dogs." *"You're right, they have more in common than not - they both have four legs and fur, they both make good pets, and they both have whiskers. On the other hand..."*

"You should be able to deliver this part in three days. You've done it before." *"You're right we have done it before, and we do need to get faster as a company. Our typical delivery time is currently five days, however, because..."*

"We deserve a discount. We give you a lot of business." *"Yes you do give us a lot of business - and you have every right to ask for a discount. In fact, we have a set of criteria for discounts and once those criteria are met, it will be my pleasure to give you a discount. Would you like to go over them now, or should I contact you once they're met?"*

"Look, I don't know when I'll have a firm delivery date for you. I'll let you know - let's just leave it at that." *"I can certainly understand your position, it's not always possible to know ahead of time when the next supply shipment will be ready. At the same time though, I'm sure you'll agree we can't tell that to our customer. Why don't I get back to you in two days and see if anything has developed? That way we have a next step to report to our customer."*

Step 3: Suggest a next step, which you can take together.

To keep momentum and keep things moving in your value stream, you and your suppliers always have to have a clear next step with a time stamp. No next step, no momentum. And without momentum, deliverables fall through the cracks and customers suffer. Similarly when dealing directly with your customers, if you don't suggest a next step, your request runs the risk of standing still. Therefore the final step in your Personal Influence plan is to offer up a next step for them to take - or preferably for both of you to take together.

EXAMPLES:

"I'm glad you agree, let's set a time to meet and plan it."

"Since it makes sense to create a lead time ordering process, let's get started. Who else do you think we should involve?"

"Okay - why don't I call you tomorrow to confirm that's been done?"

Now that you have a solid plan on what to say if you encounter objections, consider dressing it up in a nice suit for extra polish. There are three nice suits to consider:

Resistance Buster #1: Agree-Shift-Action. Agree: Acknowledge their point. Agree wherever you can. Do not argue! Shift: Change their perspective with your counterpoint and/or correct any misinformation. Action: Seek agreement and then move to conclude with a next step.

Example: *"I agree it's a bit of an inconvenience to have to purchase special data packages before every trip overseas. On the other hand, the 20 minutes it requires can save an average of $600 per trip based on your usage data on my computer Mr. Customer. All in all, not a bad investment for 20 minutes, would you agree? Great - let's set it up..."*

Resistance Buster #2: Shared Objective. One very powerful way to meet with and overcome resistance from others is to transform their objection or concern into a shared objective. The power of this technique is that it instantly moves the other person from the role of opposition to willing problem-solving partner. If they think your idea requires too many hours of work, you say, *"So our objective is to find a way to minimize the work hours we have to put in directly, do I understand?"* If the other person feels your business idea could affect service, you say, *"So our objective, then, is to ensure service isn't compromised when we implement this plan, would you agree?"* If they say, *"This committee just doesn't have room on its plate for this issue,"* then you reply, *"Then perhaps our objective is to bring it to the next meeting and decide if it's important enough to rearrange our priorities and add it to our plate, would that be fair to say?"*

Again, the power of the objection-objective technique is that it keeps you in the game - instead of getting shut out by someone's resistance, you are side-stepping it and moving the process forward.

Resistance Buster #3: Feel-Felt-Found. Another all-time great in the field of persuasion is the classic "feel-felt-found" technique. It goes like this: *"I know how you feel, a lot of people have felt the same way. What they found is..."* Each part of feel-felt-found has an important psychological function in the persuasion process. *"I know how you feel"* creates rapport and is another way of agreeing with them. *"A lot of people have felt the same way"* validates their feelings, by letting them know their resistance is normal and natural. *"What they found is"* sets them up for a reliable answer to their concern, an answer which has been good enough for others, and therefore may be good enough for them. Most people have the best success with this technique when they don't use the words feel, felt, or found. They are too recognizable to some people. Use more subtle expressions like, *"I hear you. You're not alone with that concern. What usually happens is..."*

Competency 5: Get the Right Things Done (A Supplement to Customer F.I.R.S.T.)

(This entire section is based on work by Stephen Covey, The 7 Habits of Highly Effective People, First Things First, David Allen, Getting Things Done, Peter Drucker, The Effective Executive, Andrew Groves, High Output Management, Gloria Mark, digital distraction researcher at University of California, and HBR contributors Bregman, Scwartz and Samuel.)

In order to maximize your capacity to serve your customers and colleagues, you must manage your time and prioritize your activities effectively. You can master your interpersonal skills with the Customer F.I.R.S.T. interaction system and become an interpersonal genius, but if you don't keep a written to-do list, if you waste time on unimportant activities, or work reactively all day long you can still end up forgetting deadlines, being late with deliverables and getting swept up into managing chronic emergencies all day long.

A THOUGHT EXPERIMENT

You finally win the lottery! You get $1,440 a day for the rest of your life. It's a very special payout system however, unlike anything you have ever seen before. To compensate you for winning, the lottery company takes control of your bank account. Every day $1,440 is instantly deposited in your account. You can spend all of it, some of it or none of it – regardless, at the end of your day, any remaining money in your account is deleted. Gone. The following day, you have another $1,440. Question: How hard would you work to ensure none of it is wasted? How carefully would you manage your money to ensure it ALL goes to some sort of good use and not disappear forever?

You already have this account system in place. Every day you are credited with 1,440 minutes to spend or waste as you like. At the end of each day the account is zeroed whether you spend them wisely or not - and you can never get them back. But time is not money - it's far more important than that; time is life.

Work Harder or Smarter?

Sheryl Sandberg, the CEO of Facebook, tells the ambitious to "Lean in" and assume an assertive work role, shoot for the plum assignments, assume you'll find a way to manage work and life and finally, to adopt a ferocious work ethic like hers. John Bernard advises service professionals and managers to conduct "Business at the speed of now" and tailor instant customer solutions that crush the competition, while Jack Canfield suggests we "dream about our To-Do list". If you're a salesperson or sales manager you can add advice from Michael Port who says, "Book yourself solid," or adopt the wisdom of Keith Ferrazzi and Harvey MacKay and "Never eat alone". These authors and others like them are all telling you to work harder; exert more personal energy, effort and power, thereby getting more done.

Meanwhile experts like David Allen, author of Getting Things Done, along with Harvard Business Review contributors such as Alexandra Samuel, Peter Bregman and Tony Schwartz recommend simplifying your email, getting more organized, putting things in the right "buckets", managing your energy and ritualizing or routinizing key high-value activities. These authors and experts, also highly respected and trusted advisors to organizations and individuals, are suggesting a different tack; work smarter, not harder. Could the right answer be neither of these approaches? Could the right answer instead be to do both? That decision is entirely up to you. This section of the book will show you how to work smarter and leave it entirely up to you to decide if you need to work harder.

Many Myths Abound

"I am not in control of my time. I have a reactive role." It's true that some jobs have more reactiveness built in than others. Yet no one has a *fully* reactive role. All jobs have room – and often have a clear requirement – for some degree of prevention, improvement, resourcefulness, and proactive anticipation of issues. Failing to see that will mean you miss such opportunities and are therefore less effective than another person might be in the exact same role.

"I need more time to get things done. There is simply not enough time." Certainly if we all had more time, we would have the opportunity to get more done. But we all have the same amount of time, even though we all vary in our effectiveness. The illusion of needing more time generally comes from one of two places: Poor prioritization and scheduling skills, or an unrealistic drive to accomplish "everything on my plate, and all before the end of the day."

"My job is simple - I am paid to do the things that others ask/tell me to do." All jobs certainly require us to do things for others. However, it's also true that every job is more than that. Some of the critical things you need to get done in fact don't get cued or prompted by other people. Yet they are expected to get done. Failure to see this could mean failure to achieve all your required organizational objectives.

"The more urgent something is, the higher the priority I must give it." Urgency is just one element of prioritization. The other is importance. And some things have a greater impact than others. If you prioritize by urgency, you probably waste a lot of time urgently getting things done that you shouldn't even be doing.

"Meetings are a huge time-waster for me and for this organization." Unnecessary or poorly run meetings are time wasters. Meetings by themselves are not. In fact meetings are critical to organizational effectiveness. Many teams should have more meetings, not less. But they have to be well-organized and only invite people whose contributions are required.

"Reading and responding to emails is a productive activity." 1) Not if you read emails that do not contain information to help you do your priority tasks. 2) Not if you are reading them for the wrong reasons. 3) Not if you are sending out information to others that they do not require. 4) Not if you are reading them and then procrastinating the ones that require effort and thought (email browsing).

"My job responsibilities are unclear, so I generally do whatever I'm asked to do." Some jobs are unclear, but most jobs aren't. Many people experience a slow, steady drift into other tasks and responsibilities. Revisit your roles & responsibilities documents. Revisit your performance requirements. They are your blueprint. The truth is that many of us allow other people to pull us away from that core and into new responsibilities. If this happens, consider resisting it. If you can't, revise your documents.

"There is no point in planning my day in any detail because it all changes an hour later." Most people over-estimate how much their days fall apart. Not so many as you might guess. You may need to get better at *managing* new priorities and developing greater skill in scheduling them. Schedule your day with an interruption buffer, for example.

"People should respond to my emails faster. Then I could get more done." People should respond to issues, not emails per se. Email is not an action it is a medium. And depending on the nature of the issue, it's not always the right medium, either.

"I would get more done if I weren't interrupted so much." People who aren't interrupted usually aren't needed and should therefore update their resumes. Becoming more skilled at managing interruptions is key.

"I'm one of the busiest people I know. I must be doing something right." Being busy can trick you into thinking you're being productive. They both feel the same – until the end of the day when you see what did or didn't get done. Unproductive people are often a good deal busier than their more productive counterparts. The real question should be, "What am I busy doing?"

How Highly Productive Professionals Get the Right Things Done

Productive people have been highly studied by management and productivity experts over the years. They simply get more done despite having the same available hours as everyone else. And they don't all work harder or put in more hours. But they do work smarter. The following 5 things are what they do that distinguishes them from others. These 5 things are very easy to understand, but difficult to do consistently and with excellence.

1. They determine their output – both theirs and their team's – and they continually reassess what their own and their team's required output is.

2. They update and prioritize their To-Do list for 10-15 minutes each and every day according to each task's contribution to output, as opposed to prioritizing by urgency alone. That list has a 12-month horizon. They also have a "not-to-do" list.

3. They schedule both reactive and proactive work every single day (using their To-Do list). Every day, they spend a chunk of time working on something that positively does not need to get done that day.

4. They execute their important tasks. They deliberately invest their time and energy into mostly their important To-Do list items, while consciously managing interruptions and distractions that seek to replace those things.

5. They employ email and smart devices, rather than allowing those tools to employ them, or allowing them to become the work itself.

The tools and skills that follow in this section of the book will focus on expanding each of these five keys to getting the right things done.

1. Determining Your Output.

Before we can talk about managing our time to maximize our capacity to serve customers, we have to understand what our actual output is. Authors and teachers such as Andrew Groves, Stephen Covey and Peter Drucker have defined time management as becoming more effective at contributing to output. Therefore, to be effective, the service person needs to always be thinking about how an action or task will contribute to his or her output. Your output is the output of your group plus the output of our neighboring groups. Neighboring groups are those whose output strongly affects yours, and those whose outputs are strongly affected by yours. Most people will find they have three or four neighboring groups. *In fact, you have already listed their names in your Strategic List from the last chapter.* A clear understanding of your output allows you to prioritize properly.

"The secret to mastering your time is to systematically focus on importance and suppress urgency."

- Oliver Emberton

OUTPUT CLINIC:

1. Find and clarify your formal job description. (hint: it's located somewhere in your organization, ex. Similar job posting).

   - Is it accurate? *No.*
   - Is it complete? *Not even close.*

2. Compare your formal job description to what you actually do in your day, week and month.

   - Other projects you have taken on.

- Other duties/responsibilities you have assumed.

- Which ones shall you keep? Which ones shall you try to get rid of?

3. Compare both your formal job description and your actual work to your KPIs (key performance indicators/metrics).

- Are all your projects, duties and responsibilities represented in your KPIs?

- Can you add in the ones that are missing (since they are competing for your time) so that you get recognized for them?

4. Align everything and reduce it to 4-5 key items under each of the following:

- Top 4-5 responsibilities for my external customers.

- Top 4-5 responsibilities for my internal customers/colleagues.

- Top 3-4 responsibilities for corporate.

- Top 3-4 neighboring groups (groups whose outputs are closely tied to mine).

Once complete, you'll have a clear, accurate summary of your actual output. When new tasks and activities come your way, you'll be able to more easily decide what's important and what's not. You'll start spending more time doing activities that add the most value for your customers and your company.

Lastly, it's far easier to keep 5-6 bullet points in your head than 2-3 pages of role documentation, most of which is outdated.

2. Prioritizing Your To-Do List.

Now that you're clear about your actual job output - your key roles and responsibilities - you can use that instrument to prioritize your daily, weekly, monthly and quarterly activities. Now that you know what your output is, you are ready to judge the importance of the many tasks that confront you.

IMPORTANT: Anything that contributes *significantly* to your output, in your judgment. Doing it will produce *significant* (as opposed to minor) benefits; not doing it will cause *significant* (as opposed to minor) problems. Also, anything that comes from someone on your Strategic List. You have a reciprocal relationship with these people, and helping them is a good investment in that relationship – even if the request does not directly pertain to your output.

URGENT: Anything, important or not, that must get done today (or sooner), if it's going to be done at all, because the window of opportunity/deadline is closing and you cannot create another window or move the deadline to tomorrow.

Notice that these two definitions are very different. One is about whether you'll be doing a thing or not; the other is about when it needs to be done, but only assuming you'll be doing it at all. A task can be important but not urgent, and a task can be urgent but not important. For example, there is a meeting at 3pm this afternoon. Is it urgent? Yes. It is today and not tomorrow. But is it important? Depends on your output.

Let's see what happens when we cross importance with urgency. We call the following grid The Demands Matrix. It was invented by Dwight D. Eisenhower, who famously said:

*"I have many important tasks
and few of them are urgent; I
have many urgent tasks and few
of them are important."*

The Demands Matrix

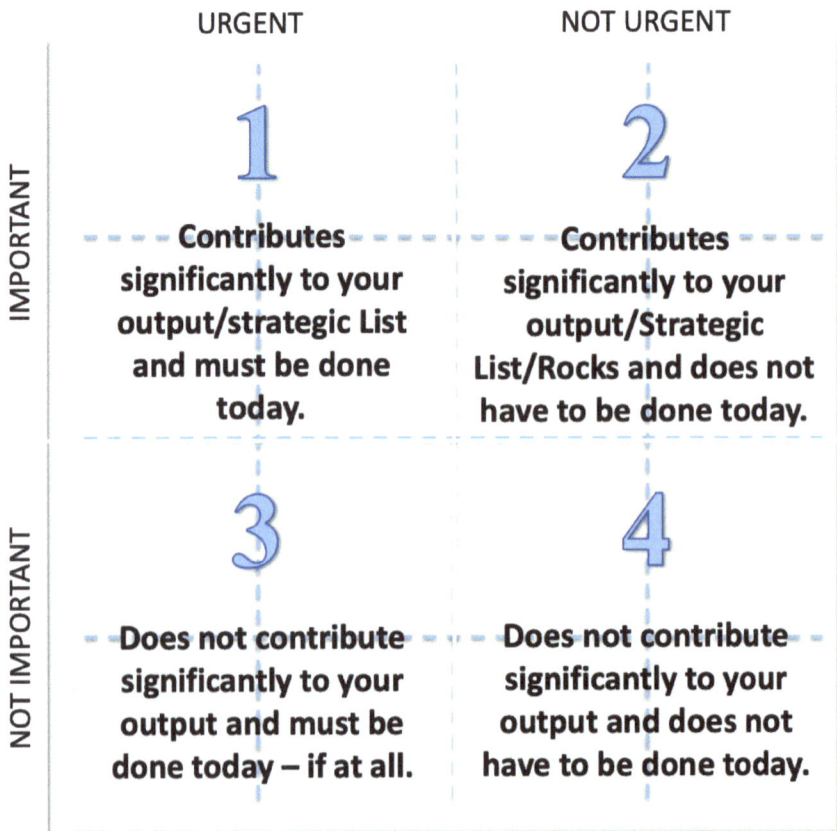

	URGENT	NOT URGENT
IMPORTANT	**1** — Contributes significantly to your output/strategic List and must be done today.	**2** — Contributes significantly to your output/Strategic List/Rocks and does not have to be done today.
NOT IMPORTANT	**3** — Does not contribute significantly to your output and must be done today – if at all.	**4** — Does not contribute significantly to your output and does not have to be done today.

QUADRANT 1 - Important tasks that must be done today, if you are in fact going to do them at all (and you should).

Examples include urgent customer issues, unforeseen emergencies, urgent deadlines, urgent management requests, crises, today's must-attend meetings, etc. Never go into Q1 without a plan on how and when you'll get out - or you probably never will. Q1 activities can consume you and distract you from Q2s. Q1 is a stressful place - and some people are addicted to it. For some people, the only activities they do are urgent ones - they can't even see an issue until it becomes urgent. Of course, some jobs by definition require you to spend 80% of your time in Q1. But 80% is not 100% - you still need to carve out slices of time to get ahead, prevent problems and make progress. That is Q2.

QUADRANT 2 - Important tasks that do not have to be done today, assuming you'll be doing them at all (but you should, at some point). Examples include planning, prevention activities, coaching/teaching, reporting, reflecting, personal and professional development, following up with customers and suppliers, relationship building and networking. Because none of these activities are urgent, it is tempting to put them off. As a result, as productive as they are, they are often neglected. Q1 means dealing with things in their crisis form; Q2 means dealing with things in their calm form.

QUADRANT 3 - Unimportant tasks that must be done today, if you are in fact going to do them at all (and you shouldn't). Some meetings, phone calls, emails and other tasks just aren't important in light of your output, and even though they are urgent, shouldn't be done at all. They take away time from your higher value Q2 and Q1 activities. But it is easy for most people to get hooked by the word "urgent." If someone says, "I need your help with something and it's urgent," it is tempting to assume it's also important. But that is not always the case.

QUADRANT 4 - Tasks that are neither important nor urgent (you should not to them, ever). Gossip, pointless complaining, email browsing, attending unimportant or poorly planned meetings, taking too long to complete a task, etc. This is the most unproductive quadrant of all. Steer clear of it at all costs.

Quadrants 1 and 2 are your To-Do list. Within that list, some things are urgent and some are not. Quadrants 3 and 4 are your Not-To-Do list. Urgent or not, the things in Q3 and Q4 just aren't important - so you shouldn't be doing them; they can eat up your time and keep you from your higher value Q1s and Q2s.

Take the Q3/Q4 Time-Waster Test

Check the ones you sometimes do. I sometimes waste time by...

__ Email browsing (scanning emails and not doing anything productive with any of them, searching through a large inbox folder trying to find a message, etc.)

__ Confusing activity with productivity (example: "We had a phone conversation about X" vs. "We made a decision to implement X by next Fri- day."

__ Doing other peoples' work just to ensure it's done or because I believe I can do it faster/better.

__ Failing to clarify the length of a requested report, and therefore making it longer/more comprehensive than perhaps necessary.

__ Prioritizing my activities by which ones are quick and easy to get off my plate.

__ Prioritizing my activities by which ones I enjoy doing most.

——

__ Prioritizing my activities by which customers or colleagues "scream the loudest".

__ Focusing on the urgency of a request and not deliberately verifying its importance.

__ Failing to verify the urgency of important requests.

__ Taking longer than necessary to complete a task (ex. making it better than anyone needs it to be).

__ Failing to schedule work that is important but not urgent, so as to complete it before it transforms into an emergency.

__ Neglecting to write everything down, causing me to sometimes forget certain commitments and deliver them a bit late.

__ Confusing relationship building conversations with pointless complaining and "opinionating".

__ Repeatedly addressing a crisis that has a clear chronic nature and which I could take action to reduce or eliminate.

__ Attending meetings which do not require my contribution.

__ Attending entire long meetings (2hrs to all day) that only require a small (10-30 minute) contribution from me.

__ Refusing or forgetting to take time to eat.

__ Refusing to take intellectual breaks that reinvigorate the mind and body and enable a fresh perspective.

__ Allowing others to take a disproportionate amount of my time to accomplish things that could be done far more quickly.

__ Saying Yes to others' requests indiscriminately, regardless of their lack of strategic relationship or the importance of the request relative to my roles and responsibilities.

__ Allowing myself to be distracted by notifications of new emails, texts, push notifications, etc. when more important work needs to get completed.

Did you check more than five items? If so, you might want to consider making changes/improvements to your current philosophy and system of personal productivity. It could be that you're spending too much time in Qs 3 and 4, at the expense of your more important tasks in Qs 1 and 2. These Q3s and 4s are your Not-To-Do list.

Only Quadrant 2 Shrinks Quadrant 1. It may seem counterintuitive at first, but the more time you spend in Q1, the bigger it becomes. People think they're making progress as they bravely push through their Q1 list, but in fact, every hour they spend in Q1 is an hour they are not spending in Q2 - the prevention quadrant. With their nose to the grindstone, they may not realize that three of the crises they're working on this afternoon actually happen every month. Without this awareness, they don't think to schedule Q2 time to create a permanent fix to the problem - a Q2 activity. In fact, it's worse than that; every neglected Q2 item can transform into as many as five different Q1 emergencies.

People in Quadrant 3 Think They're in Quadrant 1. Have you ever had a day where you were busy, busy, busy - like a ping pong ball getting passed from side to side all day? At the end of the day you were exhausted? And when you looked back on your day you thought, "I didn't even get anything done?" What quadrant were you in all day? You were in Q3. What quadrant did you think you were in? Q1. People in Q3 think they're in Q1 because they both feel the same; they are both stressful and hectic. The question you forgot to ask yourself that day was, "Urgent or not, is this thing actually important?"

"Busy is the new stupid." - Ed Baldwin

From now on, make sure every task that comes to you passes through two gates before you decide to act on it. **Gate 1:** Is it important? Urgent or not, does this thing contribute to my output significantly? If Yes, do it or schedule it. If No, ask yourself a second question: *"Is the person that's asking a member of my Strategic List? Is he from a neighboring group? Do we have a reciprocal relationship? Might I need his help with something tomorrow?"* If Yes, do it or schedule it. If No, politely say No and help them find someone whose outputs make them better suited for the task. **Gate 2:** Is it urgent? If in fact the requested task does make it through the Importance Gate, only then should you wonder about its urgency. Unless you trust the person's judgement implicitly, always verify urgency by asking questions. So, when a new task comes to you, first wonder about its importance; then wonder about its urgency. You'll be saying No a lot more.

"Productive people refuse to do the very things that average people refuse to drop." – Ken Blanchard

"Highly productive people share a secret – they have all learned to live with the constant low-level noise of the moderate disapproval of others." - Brent Finnamore

"Any time you're making something important happen, someone doesn't like you." – Tom Peters

"If everyone approves of you, you may not be doing your best work." –Michael B. Stanier

Saying No, Nicely

"I'd like to be able to help but I'm afraid my current priorities won't al- low me the time..." "...sorry about that..." "...I hope it works out for you."

"I'd like to help but with my current schedule I'd be unreliable, and I won't be that."

"I'm afraid I can't give that project the time and energy it deserves right now, but thanks for thinking of me."

"I'd like to help but my schedule is particularly full right now and I wouldn't feel comfortable deprioritizing my other tasks. I'll have to say no this time around."

"With my current priorities I've had to say No to quite a few things lately and I'm very sorry to have to add this to that list..."

"I wish I was in a position to help with this..."

3. Scheduling Reactive and Proactive Work Every Day

It's time to get your pen and paper again. **Make a list of things that, if you did them, would greatly help you to produce better results in your work.** Again, make a list of activities, tasks and projects that, if you were to do them, would help you make great progress toward your output. Make your list as long as possible. The longer your list, the more benefit you'll get from this exercise. The items you're writing are a list of things that are coming from *you*. They are not prompted by other people's requests; they are coming directly from you. They are not reactive, they are proactive. They are all very important – they will all have a significant impact on your output. And you're not currently doing them. Now you know what your current time management system is costing you.

We all know the insightful story; when big rocks are placed in a jar, is the jar full? A great deal of sand can still be put in, which falls all around the rocks. Is the jar full then? Water can be added, which fills in the small spaces between the sand. What is the lesson? Some people say the lesson is that you can always fit more things in your day. While this may be true, it is not the most important take-away from this metaphor: *If you don't put the rocks in first, you'll never fit them in.*

Now look at the list you made. Every one of them is a rock. And every one of them is a Q2. Which means they are not urgent; which is why you're not doing them. Consider the power of the things you wrote - the difference you know they would make - if only you could find the time.

Rocks are important things (tasks, activities, projects, rituals with a high contribution to output) that won't make it into your schedule unless you put them in first, and then place everything else around them. They are your "ought's" and "should's". They are prompted by you, not by others. They require initiative on your part. You must schedule them first – while there's still white space in your calendar – then defend their place when other things (sand and water) try to take their place.

Less effective people don't have any – and in fact can't even identify their rocks - because they only do reactive work prompted by others. Sand and water activities, on the other hand, are also important things, but they are prompted or requested by others. Most jobs have far more sand tasks than rock tasks.

How To Schedule Effectively

1. Schedule. Actually write things down. A mental list is not a sched- ule. Use your To-Do list and your calendar to schedule. Operate on a 12-month horizon.

2. Put your "rocks" in first. If you don't, you'll never fit them in. These are the items that are prompted by you and not by others.

3. Schedule other non-urgent work. There will be no shortage of urgent work that will come flooding in, so make sure you have already created small blocks of time for important but non-urgent work that is requested/expected/required by others.

4. **Build in an interruption buffer for walk-in's and pop-ups.** Ex. If you are interrupted by new, last-minute tasks on average 3 hrs per day, leave 3 hrs open, spread out.

Plan in the AM, Defend in the PM

Let's say you scheduled a Rock activity for 8:30AM on Thursday; if and when a customer or manager asks to see you on Thursday at 8:30AM, say, "I've got something then but how's 9?" Try this technique ten times and it will work 8. But if you simply say, "Okay" to the customer or manager and then bump your rock activity to another time without even trying to defend it, you'll quickly stop the habit of scheduling rocks in the first place - and you'll be back to old habits.

Ritualize your Week

Can you imagine swimming four kilometers, then immediately cycling 180 kilometers, then running a full marathon? This super-human feat is called the Ironman(R) triathlon. And if you think that's extraordinary, there are even deca-distances - a small handful of athletes actually race ten full Ironmans in ten days. How do they do it? How in the world do they get themselves into that kind of shape? The answer is that they have a secret: They create rituals. Every Saturday morning, they bike 4-5 hours, then run 10km - no exceptions. Every Wednesday morning, they swim for two hours then bike for one hour, etc. And contrary to popular belief, for most of these super-human athletes it does not require self-discipline; they have created rituals. For them it is automatic - there is no decision to be made.

You can accomplish great things in your work by doing the exact same thing. Take your highest-value activities and turn them into automatic habits, so that NOT getting them done becomes the exception, not the rule.

- Choose three or four high-value activities – those which have a strong contribution to output (can be Rocks).

- Grab a tiny little "corner" of time somewhere you won't likely be bothered. I.e., First thing Monday morning, Wednesday at 1:00pm, Friday at 8:00am, five minutes after staff meetings, etc.

- Form a new habit. A habit is something that has become easier to continue doing than to stop.

- Defend them. "I'm sorry, I've got something at 10:00am, is 10:30am okay, or does 11:00 work better for you?"

The Priority Talk

Sometimes your manager or your customer comes to you with an urgent issue that takes you off track. When a manager or a customer asks you to drop everything and take care of this latest urgent item, most times you can probably find a way to do it and still keep things in balance. Your years on the job have perhaps earned you that savvy. But occasionally you can't see a way to drop everything without causing damage to another customer or to some internal colleague. In such cases, The Priority Talk may help. It helps you create a positive, respectful climate where you and the other person can have a learning conversation about each other's priorities so that you can generate a superior solution together.

Step 1 - Choose the right time. That means not using the Priority Talk when your manager appears highly stressed or agitated.

Step 2 - Say, "I need your help." This means don't complain, make a request. Asking for help is never seen as negative. It engages the manager and brings her or him into the discussion.

Step 3 - Say you'll do it. It's important to quickly show your manager that you're not pushing back because you just don't feel like doing a thing, and not because you are incapable of managing your own workload. It's because you are committed to making a difference to your customers and to your company.

It reminds your manager that you're simply trying to maximize your contribution to output.

Step 4 - Share your specific commitments. Provide details as opposed to being vague and unclear. This helps your manager grasp the full picture in order to make a better decision.

Step 5 - Make a suggestion. Instead of pausing and waiting for your manager to divine a solution to the problem you've just handed them, offer a couple of alternatives so your manager can pick one or suggest another.

The Priority Talk is a learning conversation between two people. It is a climate-setting device to enable negotiation, enabling higher commitment reliability and quality. It is a way to discuss and prioritize important issues and tasks which may be in conflict. And finally, it is a way to help ensure damage is not done to the organization without mutual knowledge.

EXAMPLE:
Employee: *"I think I need your help."*

Manager: *"What's the problem, can't you take care of this? I need you to take care of this!"*

Employee: *"Yes, I can see this is serious and needs to get done. If you want me to drop everything else and do this, I will. It's just wanted to be sure we're both clear on the consequences of my dropping this item I'm working on right now...the 5 pm deadline for (customer). I need the rest of the day to get it done, and then I can take care of this issue first thing tomorrow morning."*

Manager: *"I need you to do both."*

Employee: *"Yes, of course. That's why I wanted to bring this up and get your help. I wonder if we should...(present alternatives for manager to consider, that align with his or her current priorities)...?"*

Manager: *"OK, let's go with your second option."*

Tips For Managers:

As with the Can-Sandwich and S.I.P.O.C., it's important to support your employees in using this technique with you. Even if they are incorrect in their facts, support their attempts to start a dialogue with you. There may not be any choice but to drop everything and do what you ask, but praise their efforts to help the company.

5. Execute - and Manage Interruptions.

We're back to your To-Do list again. It's time to put it all together into a system that lets you execute your tasks with consistent, repeatable effectiveness.

Your Master System

1. Put in your Rocks. Always the first thing you do as you plan your week.

2. Build/update your To-Do list of known tasks and projects.

    Then as new items arise (and they always do), ask yourself "Is this an action?" If not, dump it or store it.

3. Assign each action a quadrant ("Is it important? Is it urgent?"). Remember that your new To-Do list consists only of Q1 and Q2 activities.

4. Assign an "A" to two of the most urgent Q1s and one of the most important Q2s. Now you have A's for both quadrants.

5. Assign a "B" to the next most urgent Q1s and next most important Q2s.

6. Work your "A" items from both quadrants until they are done, or until more "A" items emerge. Then work your "B" items until more "A" items emerge.

You can also picture this system as a flowchart if you prefer. The end result will be the same. 4-D everything:

Dump it - refuse to do it.

Delegate it - give it to someone whose outputs are more aligned to the task.

Defer it - schedule a place for it to happen. Do it - get it done right now.

6. Employ Email and Smart Devices.

Take Control of your Email

The McKinsey Global Institute (2013) found highly skilled office workers spend a full quarter of their day reading, writing and sorting email.

```
                    ┌─────────────────────────┐
                    │   Look for white space  │
                    │   and put in your rocks.│
                    └─────────────────────────┘
                                 │
                                 ▼
New items           ┌─────────────────────────┐
• Projects          │ Build/update To-Do list │
• Requests          │ of known tasks/projects.│
• Meetings          │ Plan your day with      │
• Ideas             │ interruption buffer.    │
                    └─────────────────────────┘
                                 │
                                 ▼
                    ┌─────────────────────────┐
        N           │   Is it an action or    │
                    │        project?         │
                    └─────────────────────────┘
                                 │ Y
                                 ▼
┌─────────────────┐ ┌─────────────────────────┐
│  Archive it or  │ │   Is it important,      │
│  Dump it.       │ │   given your roles?     │
└─────────────────┘ └─────────────────────────┘
        N                        │ Y          ──────►  Project?
                                 │                       (plan)
┌─────────────────┐ ┌─────────────────────────┐           │
│  Dump it or     │ │    2 min. or less?      │ ◄───────  Actions
│  Delegate it (to│ └─────────────────────────┘
│  someone whose  │              │ N            │ Y
│  roles are      │
│  aligned with it).│
└─────────────────┘ ┌─────────────────────────┐
                    │      Is it urgent?      │
                    └─────────────────────────┘
                       Y         │ N
                                 │
┌─────────────────┐ ┌──────────────────┐ ┌──────────────┐
│ Q1, assign A, B,│ │ Q2, assign A, B, │ │   Do it.     │
│ Defer it → Do it.│ │ Defer it → Do it.│ └──────────────┘
└─────────────────┘ └──────────────────┘
```

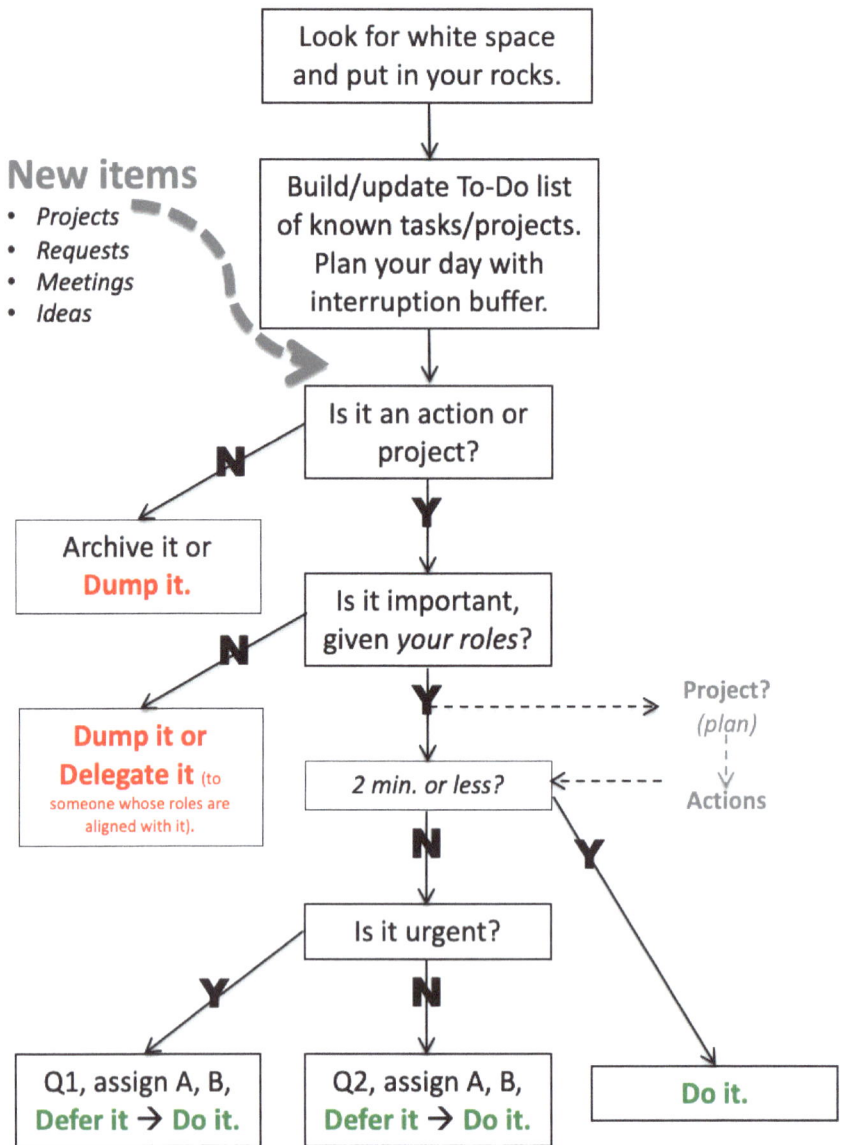

Management and productivity experts say we generate emails because it requires little effort or thought. Compared to other activities like walking to another floor for an F2F, playing phone tag for days before having a V2V, attending a 2-hr meeting where only 20 min. pertains to you, or digging in to a project that requires creative and concentrated thought, shooting off a few emails is a very attractive way to look and feel busy.

- Clear out your in-box. Set up three folders: "My Actions", "Commitments to me" and "Archive". If you have anything that can't fit in one of these three folders, it probably needs to be deleted. If you are a salesperson, add a fourth folder: "Prospects/Customers".

  "My Actions" is your email To-Do list.

  "Commitments to me" is your tracking of other people's commitments to you, which you need to follow on and set gates and dates.

  "Archives" is a folder for messages you are done with, but want to retain for your records.

  "Prospects/Customers" is your folder for current issues categorized by your key accounts. If it involved United Airlines, you can find it there.

- Manage your in-box in batches. Depending on your work role, turn off the "ding!" and instead consider checking your email at your own prompting. Every hour, or even as rarely as twice per day.

- Condition your contacts to use the right medium. Let colleagues (even customers) know that if they have an urgent issue they should call you instead of emailing. Ask people to not include you in their cc list unless they're sure you need to know. Tell them to underline the action they are requesting. Tell them to put the issue and the ask in the subject window.

- Create an email signature that includes this message:

  Join the fight against excessive email.

  • Focus on your priorities – I'll understand if you don't reply right away.

  • Please know I'm checking emails regularly, even if I don't reply immediately, I'm working your issue!"

  • If it's urgent reach me by phone 555-5555.

Take Control of your Smart Phone

Smart devices are sometimes empowering. They put a world of information at your fingertips. They free people up from having to be at an office computer or even a home computer to communicate and re- search info. We can be productive anywhere.

Now, the Bad News. Ofcom, Britain's telecommunications regulator, found 60% of surveyed teenage smartphone users describe them- selves as "highly addicted". So do 37% of adults. Not long ago, doc- tors were the only ones on call all the time. Then came pagers – and people felt like slaves to them. With smartphones, we're all on call 24/7 - with our new "pagers". Bosses think nothing of invading people's free time. Work invades home more than domestic chores invade the office. People check their smartphones obsessively, displaying drug-like addiction behaviors. Surveys repeatedly show that large numbers of smartphone addicts check messages more than 100 times per day – even at midnight when they should be sleeping, or on Christmas morning before opening presents. It's all very distracting, and it creates a dilemma between what constitutes real work and "make work".

People think more deeply if they are not constantly distracted. Try these tips to tame the smartphone beast:

- Set "Airplane mode" as default.

- Do not, do not, do not check your phone during meetings. Boring meeting? Why are you there?!

- Adopt a "snack food" mentality and policy. No one eats Doritos all day.

- Monitor your activity vs. productivity index. How much of your smart- phone use during work time is actually contributing to your output? Busy isn't the same as productive.

- Be judicious with push notifications.

- Let it enhance your personal life, but don't let it invade your work life.

MIT Sloan Research Reviews on Multitasking

Andrea Ichino and Nicola Persico studied a group of judges who were randomly assigned cases and who had similar workloads in terms of the quantity and type of cases they were assigned. They found the judges who worked on fewer cases at a time tended to complete more cases per quarter and took lees time on average to complete each case (National bureau of Economic Research, W16502, "Don't Spread Yourself Too Thin. The Impact of Task Juggling on Speed of Job Completion.").

Sinan Aral, Erik Brynjolfsson and Marshall Van Alstyne studied information workers and found working on more projects at a time at first increased productivity as measured by revenue generation. But as the level of multitasking increased, the marginal benefits of additional multitasking decreased sharply. Then, taking on still more tasks made workers less productive rather than more so. The researchers suggest that excessive multitasking results in the workflow equivalent of a traffic jam (2008 MIT Sloan Management Review, 49212).

In another study conducted by Robert Rogers and Stephen Monsell, participants were slower when they had to switch tasks than when they repeated the same task. (Rogers, R. & Monsell, S. (1995). *The costs of a predictable switch between simple cognitive tasks.* Journal of Experimental Psychology: General, 124, 207-231).

Another study conducted in 2001 by Joshua Rubinstein, Jeffrey Evans and David Meyer found that participants lost significant amounts of time as they switched between multiple tasks and lost even more time as the tasks became increasingly complex. (Rubinstein, Joshua S.; Meyer, David E.; Evans, Jeffrey E. (2001). Executive Control of Cognitive Processes in Task Switching. Journal of Experimental Psychology: Human Perception and Performance, 27(4), 763-797).

Practical Applications for Multitasking Research

Meyer suggests that productivity can be reduced by as much as 40 percent by the mental blocks created when people switch tasks. Now that you understand the potential detrimental impact of multitasking, you can put this knowledge to work to increase your productivity and efficiency. The next time you find yourself multitasking, take a quick assessment of what you are trying to accomplish. Eliminate distractions and try to focus on one task at a time.

More tips & techniques for getting the right things done:

- Plan your day in 15 minute chunks like lawyers and accountants do. Then strive to create value in every chunk.

- Take advantage of mental momentum – organize classes of tasks where possible (calls, emails, report writing) together.

- Notice where you're losing small bits of time - 5 min. here, 6 min. there – and use them for quick actions (follow-ups, etc.).

- Handle small items in real time wherever possible. Use the 2 minute rule: If you can do it in 2 minutes or less, don't schedule it, just do it.

- Parkinson's Law – work will expand to fill the time allocated; work will also contract to fit the time allocated. Try to do things in smaller and smaller chunks of time.

- Do the things other people do at times when they don't do them. This reduces queuing time.

- Be efficient with things/projects; be effective with people/customers. If you try to be efficient with people, you'll treat them like things.

- When simply sending data use email; when trying to influence use F2F or V2V.

- Meet with talkative time-wasters 5 min. before they have to be some- where. Always go to them, so you can leave.

- Have an interruption management strategy – make it hard to sit, say Yes, I have 2 minutes, and stand to meet unscheduled people.

- Screen your meetings – ask, Is there an agenda? What do you want me to contribute? How long is the meeting scheduled to last? No agenda, no "attenda."

- Try to check email less often (if roles permit) – strive for 4 times per day. Remove distracting alerts.

- Ask yourself the Power Question several times each day: What can I do, right this minute, to make this day highly productive?

- K.I.S.S. your emails and reports. Keep It Short and Simple.

- Never go into Q1 without a clear strategy on how and when you will get out – or you'll never get out.

- Set aside what Jack Welch calls "Window gazing time" to plan, reflect and see the bigger picture.

- Always invest unexpected "extra" time (from a cancelled meeting) in Q2 activities, not in Q1.

- Resist the urge to always do everything to the very best of your ability. You may create wasted, unnecessary value that doesn't contribute to output.

- Confirm or verify (politely) all so-called urgent requests from col- leagues and customers. Get more specific than ASAP.

- Take breaks – your brain requires them, and will take them anyway.

- Get up from your chair at least every 45 min. and walk around for a minute – to the fountain, to the washroom, to the window. It revitalizes your mind and helps your ergonomics.

- Always put the issue and the ask in the subject window of emails. Consider putting the deadline too. Ask others to do the same in their emails.

- When sending a chain of emails, briefly explain the situation – don't make the other person spend 10 min. on detective work.

- Do not hit Reply All unless each and every person in the list requires your response.

- Use cc only to share information that others need to do their job. Don't cc to show off or to try and get another person to act.

- Leave detailed voicemails – with enough information for the other per- son to do something before speaking to you next.

- Do not keep mental lists – write every to-do down instead so you can focus on other things and experience less stress.

- Do a weekly review – every Friday afternoon or Monday morning gather up everything that is pending/incomplete and assess. Then 4- D each item (dump it, delegate it, defer it or do it).

- Go for a 15-20 min. walk every day at lunchtime. Don't think – just do it...you'll be amazed at what happens.

- Offer help, but don't own OPW (other peoples' work).

- Relationship-building is Q2 – it is important and productive. It is not a Q3 or a Q4 activity.

- Handle things once. Emails, documents, etc. Don't waste time skimming repeatedly.

Implementing Customer F.I.R.S.T. In Your Organization

Not Training; Culture Change

Customer First is a human and organizational capital improvement program designed to improve intangible asset readiness and impact financial and non-financial metrics. It drives new, widespread behaviors throughout the organization. It is therefore a culture change program. Fundamentally, successful culture change requires the common sense of experienced management. In her book, "Unleash Behaviors, Unlock Profits," author L. W. Braksick describes corporate culture as "The behaviors that are rewarded and punished by your people and your systems." With this definition alone it becomes clear that training by itself - while critical - does not cause a change in corporate culture, nor can you expect to impact key metrics through training alone. Retaining knowledge is just as important as learning it. Transferring it to the daily job is just as important as retaining it. Deep change requires strong, clear leadership behavior change and new policies and practices. Think how much damage is done when an executive says, "Don't use that Can-Sandwich crap on me, just get it done."

Improving how your company creates and delivers its value proposition to its customers requires changes in specific organizational capacities, and that requires some fine-tuning of company culture. In the first part of this book, we introduced front-line skills needed for customer service excellence. Organizational capacities are a function of skills, policies and metrics all working together in alignment. Skills are taught through training and coaching. Organizational capacities are developed through improvement programs aimed at precise culture change.

Examples of skills: Active listening, negotiating win-win agreements, selling premium priced solutions, making reliable commitments to customers.

Examples of organizational capacities: Delivering on time, continuous improvement, sales & operations planning, delighting customers profitably.

The Implementation Steps - The 3-I's

The 3-I's represent the contributions companies need to make in order to realize significant returns on their investment in Customer First - or any improvement initiative. Our team at The Finnamore Group adapted this framework from a variety of best practices, including the Change First philosophy (Implementation vs. Installation) and work by Trice and Bellers (1993), The Cultures of Work Organizations, identifying stages of changing a workplace culture: Adopt, Implement, Institutionalize.

Install - Installation means installing new skills and tools into the organization. This is achieved through training—ideally through a combination of classroom and on-line. Managers and employees receive training and coaching on new behaviors, new skills, new methods. The company contributes by giving permission to learning provider.

Integrate - Integration means integrate the tools with existing systems and structures in order to make them a permanent part of the organization's way of working. The new behaviors, tools and skills are merged with existing processes, structures and tools. The company contributes by taking action and making changes.

Institutionalize - Institutionalization means making the skills and tools become new behavioral norms to the point where not doing them makes you stand out as odd. Everyone adjusts to new behaviors and develops new beliefs about how to do their work. The company contributes by making deeper changes in its leadership methods and its performance management structures.

ROI

We like to talk with our clients about return on investment. It surprises some of our clients that there are in fact three levels of return they can choose.

Return on installation – minimal benefits, usually temporary.

Return on integration – moderate benefits, often measurable.

Return on institutionalization – substantial, long-term, measurable improvements.

Kotter's 8 Steps of Change

John Kotter's 8 Steps (Leading Change, 2012) plus the 3-I's give us the change agenda.

1. Establish a sense of urgency and a burning platform.

2. Form a powerful guiding coalition to steer the change.

3. Create a compelling vision or end-state.

4. Communicate the vision to everyone.

5. Empower and enable others to act on the vision at every level.

6. Plan for and create short-term wins to maintain momentum.

7. Leverage early wins and create more change.

8. Institutionalize the new behaviors.

Satisfy or delight? Meet or exceed expectations?

Step three in Kotter's 8 Steps is to create a compelling vision. To that end, consider this question: How far should you go? As an executive you need to decide that either with or for your team. Let's say your current mantra is to "Continually strive to exceed customer expectations." That's an inspiring statement. It sets a bar for people to use as a standard. But what if your department's improvement rate is too slow to allow this exceeding of expectations to occur without constantly expediting? In that case, you have a mission that you can't keep up with, except by shooting yourself in the foot. Another approach many companies use is to have a target of 8.5 out of 10 on customer feedback. That's a great and specific target - but it's not a vision. It's a way to measure progress toward a vision.

Whatever the vision, it needs to a) support the company's overall strategy and b) be supported by clear metrics and targets. Let's suppose you and your management team create a vision for customer service that reads, "To be known by our customers and our prospects as the most dependable service provider in our entire industry." That's an excellent vision. And suppose your metric is an average score on a specific feedback tool of 9 out of 10. Very specific. And suppose your company's strategy is to penetrate a new market who requires, among other things, dependable promises from suppliers. This is the kind of tight alignment you must create in order to give your Customer First program clarity, focus and intensity.

Full Executive Support

It surprises some people to learn that the single greatest barrier to improving the company through culture change is not budget or human resource requirements. After all, when a clear return on investment can be seen, funding becomes more manageable. The single greatest barrier is something other than funding. It tends not to show at first, but surfaces approximately 33-50% of the way into the program – it is the manager's unwillingness to even consider the possibility that some of their most cherished behaviors and practices are contributing to the current problems in the business. "I'll have to stop doing X? I always do X. X is really important. I built my success on X. I can't give up X." And so it goes. The improvements the company desperately need never happen. The well-intended manager continues to unintentionally damage the organization with his or her cherished behavior and the new behaviors – which would improve processes and increase sustained shareholder value - cannot take hold. And yet, executive behaviors are the very key to transformation on the front lines. It is a dynamic perhaps best illustrated by a pumpkin seed in a mason jar. You can take a pumpkin seed and put it in a mason jar, and you'll get a mason jar shaped pumpkin. Don't blame the pumpkin seed - blame the mason jar. The pumpkin seed is the person; the mason jar is the environment, which is shaped exclusively by the behaviors, policies and measures set out by the executive team. The executive team sets and maintains the priorities of the organization by what they reward, punish, and communicate. More generally, by how they hire, fire, and promote. Executive buy-in means the senior management team is committed to becoming customer focused to such a degree that they are willing to change how people are managed and how they manage as individuals and as a team.

There are four levels of executive support necessary for a successful Customer First improvement initiative:

1. Investing. Investing in the consulting firm or allocating a team of your top talent to work on it one week each month for two or three years.

2. Showing up. Attending all the required meetings to show support, and having a strong presence at these meetings.

3. Modeling the new behaviors. Using them yourself as you work with colleagues and customers, and allowing the behaviors to be used with you in normal daily business.

4. Changing the organization. Where necessary, championing changes in policies and systems that currently work against the objectives the executives selected for Customer First. They can be as far-reaching as IC, sales and operations planning processes, performance management and a variety of metrics.

All four levels of support are required to create a customer focused company that delivers its value proposition at a world-class level. Nothing short of a willingness to make small but strategic changes to the organization will be required to create an environment where profitable customer-oriented behavior is encouraged, measured and rewarded.

Willingness to change the organization includes having clear firm answers to these questions: What will it mean if people don't attend the manager group coaching sessions or the training? How will it affect their careers? What will it mean when people do attend the training and coaching events? How will it be factored into their advancement? What will it mean when an executive or a GM routinely makes decisions to favor short-term cash at the expense of long-term customer satisfaction?

B=(PE) - The Implementation Model

Behavior is a function of the person and their environment. B=(PE). To change people's behavior requires training the person, but also changing the environment. The key components of Customer First that help executives change the environment are the Impact Team, the FLASH training sessions, the manager group coaching sessions and the Executive Alignment Sessions.

1. The Impact Team & Project Team

Impact Team is a steering committee composed of the stakeholders who will be strongly affected by the customer service improvement program and/or have a key role in its success. At a minimum, they should be executives and managers from key strategic groups such as HR, operations, communications, customer service, quality, finance and sales.

They should meet quarterly to review milestones, solve problems and communicate successes to the company. The Impact Team, along with the executive sponsor and the Project Team, are the key to the program's success. The field activity leaders - whether internal employees or external consultants - who are conducting the training and coaching components should report to this team quarterly.

They should meet at least once per quarter in an Impact Team Meeting. They also should attend either the FLASH sessions or the 2-day regular length course each phase as its delivered to their people. Additional meetings should take place without the consulting firm as well, if one is being used. Team members align priorities, address problems, seize opportunities and steer the improvement initiative toward maximum success. They clarify the mission. They manage corporate communication. They establish clear metrics and targets for the Customer First program. They manage the three phases of cultural change needed to improve the customer focus of the organization. They make recommendations based on feedback from the field.

The Project Team should consist of a key program CF Coordinator and their boss. The CF Coordinator is ideally a well-experienced manager who is well-known in the company. She or he needs to have their workload adjusted throughout the duration of the program to allow an average of one full day per week to be dedicated to the program's requirements. A 500 person intervention will involve no fewer than 150 significant events which need to be planned, scheduled, communicated and attended by busy people who each have good reasons not to go. The CF Coordinator is automatically a member of the Project Team, but should also be on the Impact Team. He or she should manage the administration of the program - a considerably complex task. Following are some of the more important roles and responsibilities of the CF Coordinator that will help reduce the chance of oversights, mistakes and misalignments, while simultaneously assuring maximum synergy, alignment and flawless execution of all activities related to implementation of the Solution.

1. Coordinate deployment & collection of assessments, coordinate focus groups and other information gathering activities.

2. Communicate information to facilitate correct assignment of participants to seminars, coaching groups, etc. (roles & responsibilities of target participants, number of participants, etc.).

3. Manage CF event logistics (venue arrangements, accommodations for trainers, on-site AV requirements, start times, breaks, etc.).

4. Communicate all training/coaching schedules and activities to all involved and participating parties in a reasonable, proactive time frame.

5. Confirm all schedules with involved participants before confirming dates with the external consultant assisting with CF (if applicable).

6. Participate in Impact Team meetings and record all commitments.

7. Maintain an updated Calendar of Events. This Calendar must be communicated to all Impact Team members and to the external consultant, if one is being used.

8. Remind and hold accountable appropriate people to execute their respective steps in Calendar of Events. Remind managers to ensure they and their people attend their assigned classes and coaching sessions.

9. Confirm all communiques, dates, announcements related to the solution with external consultant before publishing or sending, to allow us to provide feedback and/or add value.

10. Keep external consultant informed of any new processes or systems that relate to the topics/subjects of the solution (new roles & responsibilities, new structuring of work, new management outcome requirements, work methods, etc.), provide PowerPoints, charts and other documents related to these changes used internally.

11. Send out timely communications and notices to employees, managers and executives as required by CF.

Working Effectively with An External Consultant:

Unless your company is fortunate enough to already possess strong in-house talent for managing change and corporate culture transformation, it may be best to involve an expert with experience with your industry, and from a wider variety of industries and best practices. Of course there's a cost, but there's also a cost to a company for doing it themselves. Every organization must decide which cost is more profitable.

It's not productive to hire a consultant if the entire team is not willing to follow their advice. There's a story about a financial planner with 20 years' experience who met with her new client, helping him through a proven process to determine the best asset allocation plan for his risk tolerance and fifteen-year financial plan. The client greatly respected her experience and expertise and took her advice fully. After two years however he came to her with bits and pieces of news articles and scattered fragments of advice he had heard here and there from a variety of sources. He told her to change his portfolio according to what he now knew. She strongly advised him not to and attempted to explain her reasons, but he would not have it; after all he now had two years' experience. Within three years he dropped her as a financial planner because he didn't like the performance of the portfolio he had with her. She shook her head, dumbfounded by the idea that an intelligent man like her client could think a couple of years of hacking in a professional discipline could trump two decades of expertise.

Like a financial planner, the consultant's advice must be heeded by the client—in this case, the company, it's employees, its management and its Project Team. The relationship between the consultant and the Project Team should be a collaborative one. They are strategic partners working together to serve their mutual customer - the company and the executive sponsor. Accordingly, the consultant should report to the executive sponsor.

Executive Education, Alignment & Support

FLASH Training for Executives

In order to set a strong example, executives need to be able to model the customer-focused behaviors being installed across the company. Also, they need to be aware of the principles and tools being implemented so that they reinforce and support them, and so they don't accidentally contradict them in their daily work and during critical crisis moments. The first questions that are asked in Customer F.I.R.S.T. training courses by employees are, predictably, "Did you teach this to my boss?" and "Are you sure my boss approves of me doing things in this new way?" To this end, executives should be exposed to a brief "FLASH" version of the training curriculum for Customer F.I.R.S.T. 1 and 2. Following the FLASH, they should communicate their understanding and their support to their people. All executives and directors should attend the one-day FLASH version of the Customer F.I.R.S.T. two-day courses. During the FLASH sessions, each tool or skill is explained, followed by a discussion about what it will look like when everyone uses the given tool, and how to best support the use of it by employees. NOTE: Many of these tools require significant behavior change and may mean a shift in your culture. Rather than surface techniques, most of the Customer F.I.R.S.T. tools are deep, far-reaching behavioral patterns which require leadership support. As an executive, your support of CF is crucial in your transition to an increasingly customer-centric organization.

Executive Alignment Sessions

Executives need to be aligned with one another regarding CF. They also need to get feedback on progress from the field and make decisions that support the program's progress. Generally the easiest way for this to take place is through regular periodic contact with the external consulting organization. Executive Alignment Sessions (EAS) are a series of 60-90 minute sessions with key executives. EAS's take place during all three phases of the program. Invitees include the SVP, VPs, and GMs whose people are involved in the customer service improvement program, and whose support is needed for the program to be successful. The basic EAS agenda includes continually realigning focus on customer experience improvement and improvement of dependable commitments, realigning focus on pursuit of profitable customer satisfaction, receiving and discussing feedback from the field, making recommendations based on feedback, and selecting feedback items to address as improvement projects.

Manager Education & Support

The Leadership Offsite

Service managers wonder, What's the program all about and how does it work? What's the burning platform? What's the compelling Vision? How will it affect my people and me? A leadership offsite – usually tied into an existing offsite schedule – is both a practical and a powerful way to get started on a strong foundation by introducing the initiative, gaining management input and support, and ensuring consistent messaging about the initiative to all managers. As we've explored repeatedly throughout this section, a key element of success in any initiative is management support and communication. Without it, an enabling environment may not develop and the initiative's momentum begins to fade within 6-8 months. In addition, employees may arrive at training classes unprepared and uninformed, and remain skeptical and hesitant to apply what they've learned in the training. On the other hand, when participants are well prepared and they see active management support, they enter a training session eagerly, with positive expectations, ready and able to derive maximum value from the experience. In addition, managers themselves are more willing to do their part to create a supportive, conducive environment where people can use the new tools and skills. A leadership offsite is a practical way to launch a culture-change initiative with just the right impact.

Leading First Workshop

In addition to their supportive roles, managers need to be coaches and guides for employees as they apply the Customer F.I.R.S.T. tools and skills learned in the training classes. Training means behavior change. Behavior change requires coaching and reinforcement. Without that kind of reinforcement and support, the skills learned in the training courses tend to fade rapidly and the needed behavioral changes never take hold. Training transfer – on-the-job daily application – can suffer. In addition to coaching employees, managers need to integrate the tools and skills of Customer F.I.R.S.T. into their staff meetings, performance management systems and improvement processes. The Leading First Workshop is designed to teach leadership and coaching skills to support employees' use of the tools and skills. All managers whose direct reports attend the courses should be required to attend the Leading First course.

3Rs – Relentless, Routine Review System

3Rs are quick (5-15 minutes), simple group activities to review and remind employees of Customer First tools and skills, keeping them refreshed and top-of-mind for everyone. There are 24 tools and skills comprising the entire Customer F.I.R.S.T. training program. The 3R's process cycles through them, one at a time, repeatedly. "Relentless" implies that these review activities are never, ever skipped for the sake of time, and that they will be conducted perpetually. "Routine" implies steady, consistent, predictable calendar cadence. Every Thursday for the first 10 minutes of the staff meeting, for example. This routine rhythm turns the 3Rs into a ritual. Managers can perform a review themselves or delegate it, after having led a few sessions first. If delegating, they may choose to tell/suggest which tools to review and give the employee the toolkit to choose a review activity.

Company-wide education

Customer F.I.R.S.T. Skill Building Courses

Customer facing and front-line supporting employees should all attend three phases of live classroom/virtual training where they learn the skills explained in the first part of this book: How to deal with customers, handle complaints, manage expectations, build relationships, create dependable action plans, manage time and work more effectively within service delivery processes. The courses are usually developed and conducted by external instructors with expertise in the tools and skills of the Customer F.I.R.S.T. system, and fully customized to the situations in which people work and the processes of your company. The training curriculum needs to roll out over three phases so there's time for reflection and practice of the tools learned. In phase 1 the focus should be on the skills and tools of the Customer F.I.R.S.T. interaction system. In phase 2 the emphasis can shift to self-management and supplier performance across value chains and improving influence skills. In phase 3 the focus should be on skills mastery through practice simulations and service manager coaching skills. The three phases of training should be attended by all customer facing employees, those at the second level who support customer-facing employees, and of course their managers.

A Set of Service Standards

Developing a set of standards is a powerful way to establish an executive-approved set of guidelines for managing, decision making and generally serving customers throughout the organization. Anyone who has a customer needs to be operating by the same service standards as everyone else. Only in this way can consistently reliable service ever emerge. Developed during part of the phase 3 classes, these standards are then integrated into one master set for everyone. Standards act like a lighthouse; they tell the ship captain where to go, but they leave it up to her to decide how. Examples:

1. **I Take Ownership.** Seeing a service through to its conclusion is not someone else's job; it is mine. I take it upon myself to take action. I take it upon myself to get answers. I take it upon myself to find options. I always follow up and I always follow through.

2. **I Provide the Highest Standard of Service.** I always ask myself if this answer or this option would be good enough for me if I was the customer. I always ask myself if this response timeframe would be good enough for me if I was the customer. My tone and manner is always professional, respectful and helpful.

3. **I Am Trustworthy.** I always provide accurate information; I never guess. I never over- or under-promise. I always make some kind of commitment, and only ones I know I can keep. Then I keep them.

4. **I Provide Proactive, Useful Updates.** I inform customers before they have to ask. My updates are insightful and provide more information than my customers can get from simply reading a spreadsheet. I anticipate questions and concerns and am ready to address them.

In the end, the service standards can be used by everyone because they are built by everyone.

Customer First Instructional Videos

An online program can also be a useful supplement to in-class training. While there is no substitute for in-person training when teaching interpersonal skills - the discussions and role plays cannot be fully realized with online training, however sophisticated the program may be - online training makes sense for non-customer facing staff in the organization so that they can be exposed to the CF program and the Customer F.I.R.S.T. tools, but still not have to take part in person in three 2-day classes. An online program also creates an excellent refresher for class alumni. Finally, an online program works in synergy with the manager's Coach's Toolkit to help refresh alumni and to orient new hires in the future.

Perpetual Peer-to-Peer Coaching

Peer-to-Peer Coaching is a simple way to create an environment of mutual learning and support among training alumni. By taking turns observing how a colleague has a conversation or meeting with a customer and then giving feedback, two important things happen: The coachee receives valuable feedback on how they are doing and the coach gets a valuable experience in watching the performance of their teammate and providing that feedback. Both learn and grow. Below are some sample points to build a checklist that suits your industry:

1. Was friendly and began with a polite greeting.

2. Appears to have anticipated questions and concerns and was prepared with answers.

3. Appears to have confirmed and verified current progress/status to ensure his/her information was accurate.

4. Report was insightful and useful to customer, not just reading the status update notes.

5. Was creative and innovative in developing options for the customer.

6. Found brief moments to build or maintain the relationship.

7. Was able to sense concern in the customer and was able to reassure them.

8. Always made some kind of commitment when asked, and those commitments were reliable – he/she did not overpromise or guess.

9. Delivered potentially unpleasant news neutrally, and in the best light possible.

10. When requesting actions to be taken by the customer, explained reasons and benefits for the action so that the customer was willing to act.

11. Was able to manage expectations and did so in a way that was well-received by the customer.

12. Was flexible and accommodating in their communication style in order to create rapport.

13. If customer was upset, was able to calm them down and regain trust.

14. Was helpful, responsive and professional overall.

15. Ended with a summary of decisions and actions to ensure understanding.

16. Thanked the customer for their business or otherwise expressed appreciation.

17. At the end of the call the customer was A) More at ease, B) less at ease, C) same.

18. Additional comments.

Remember – the goal is to grow together. This is a positive, supportive process. Results are not to be stored and are not sent to managers or used to assess overall performance. Once the colleague has been given feedback, notes should be deleted (if they were taken electronically).

The Complete Step-By-Step Process

The following steps closely mirror Kotter's 8 Steps and our own 3-I's of successful culture change.

Step 1 - Impact Team pre-meeting - A group of potential Impact Team members conducts a meeting wherein the dynamics, the elements and the mechanics of the Customer First program are presented. Attendees are then asked for their commitment to join the Impact Team.

Step 2 - Leadership Offsite - Conduct with entire leadership team under the SVPs whose departments are involved in the program. Invite all executives, GMs, directors and managers. Show them the overview and mechanics briefly and get their commitment to support the program. Determine compelling vision and burning platform.

Step 3 - Hold the First Impact Team Meeting. Establish mission, functions, responsibilities and working relationships. Establish Project Team and CF Coordinator. Start metrics plan. Start communication plan. Start curriculum plan for classes: CF1 Customer and supplier management, CF2 Advanced customer and supplier management plus self-management, CF3 Follow-up and Practice through simulations.

Step 4 - Schedule an Executive FLASH of CF1. Invite all executives, GMs and directors. Overview of key tools, discuss plans to support them.

Step 5 - Begin Customer F.I.R.S.T. 1 classes for employees and managers. Pre-work: All participants watch instructional videos for phase 1.

Step 6 - Hold 2-3 Executive Alignment Sessions throughout the delivery of phase 1. Report feedback from field and recommendations for changes.

Step 7 - Hold 2-3 Impact Team Meetings throughout the delivery of phase 1. Address scheduling issues for classes, communicate milestones throughout company. Plan phase 2 transition.

Step 8 - Schedule an Executive FLASH of CF2. Invite all executives, GMs and directors. Overview of key tools, discuss plans to support them.

Step 9 - Begin Customer F.I.R.S.T. 2 Classes for employees and managers who have taken CF1. Pre-work: All participants watch instructional videos for phase 2.

Step 10 - Conduct 2-3 EAS's during phase 2. Ongoing improvement project management.

Step 11 - Schedule 2-3 ITMs during phase 2. Address scheduling issues, check for progress on target metrics, communicate milestones throughout company.

Step 12 – Train all managers with the Leading First Workshop.

Step 13 - Begin Customer F.I.R.S.T. 3 Classes. In-depth simulations for mastery of CF1 & 2 skills, input into Service Standards.

Step 14 – Managers begin 3R's – Relentless, Routine Reviews.

Step 15 – Roll out Perpetual Peer-to-Peer Coaching.

For more detail on these steps and specific agendas, contact The Finnamore Group.

Executive Summary Key Principles from Customer F.I.R.S.T.

1. The goal is to delight customers profitably through mostly standard work.

2. The greatest asset in an enterprise is the customer who is being delighted profitably by highly engaged people who serve the customer through mostly normal operations.

3. Try not to overcommit. Overcommitting leads to either 1) failure, or 2) the need to expedite (which often means doing harm to HS).

4. Try not to make commitments on other peoples' behalf. If its not your process, don't promise on behalf of others. You may look good to the customer in that moment, but in the end you run the risk of either 1) failing to meet the commitment, or 2) meeting it but doing harm to HS.

5. Do not volunteer to expedite. Watch out for the unconscious habit of putting a rush on everything – AND for failing to validate a rush in the first place.

6. Do not buffer upstream (to suppliers). It's one thing to add a very small buffer to your customer, but when you buffer upstream to a supplier and exaggerate the requirement that's another thing altogether. Called lying.

7. Expectations aren't needs. Don't assume customer expectations are the same as actual business needs. Verify.

8. Strive for 80/20. Try to have 80% of your work be done as standard work/normal operations, and 20% of your work be rushed/expedited work.

9. Don't pass your stress on to others. Do not threaten or otherwise coerce others into telling you what you want to hear.

10. Be nice. The Jerk Principle: No one works harder than a jerk, because no one wants to help them. Keep your leg down. Stress makes people rush and/or turns them into jerks.

11. A customer is anyone who needs something from you. Period.

12. Everyone has customers. Everyone's job has some degree of

    impact on the external customer's experience.

13. The word "commitment" must be held as high as "quarterly profits" and "customer delight". It must be revered and always taken with the utmost seriousness. Commitments can never be requested, offered or agreed on lightly. Precision is the key to commitment-making. Explicit result, precise timeline. Vagueness leads to dropped commitments and missed dates.

14. Mutual accountability for commitment agreements. When you work with a supplier-colleague to develop a plan of action/ commitment, both parties are accountable for its completion, not just your colleague. When in doubt, you must have a "Convince me" conversation.

15. Pressure should only come from the actual, authentic need of the customer organization that is making the request. The use of yelling or threats should not contribute to the urgency you transmit to your colleagues. Even the initial request itself should rarely be taken at face value and used as a source of pressure on your network of colleagues. Dig as deeply as you can to discover the true business requirement – often different than the initial request.

16. T.E.A.M.S. is "truth-serum" for both you and your supplier- colleague. It is for use by service professionals who do not simply want the supplier to tell them what they want to hear, but rather to work with suppliers to

determine true capacity and the most realistic delivery plan – one that includes gates and dates.

17. Never go to a customer without options, and always be at least 80-90% confident in each of them. Even at 90% confidence, you are relying 10% on hope.

18. Networking helps you do better work. Build relationships with key suppliers, managers and colleagues before you need them.

19. Your ability to influence others is priceless. Work on it with a deliberate plan. Apply your influence skills to your customers and your colleagues-suppliers in order to influence the flow of value.

20. Relationship building means getting to something about each other on a personal level. It is completely appropriate when done within the comfort zone of each party.

21. To influence others, get to know what they care about most and what they want to avoid most. Then show them how your requested action helps them get what they want and avoids what they don't want.

22. Resistance is a normal, natural step in the persuasion process, whether with customers or colleagues. Anticipate arguments and counterpoints then plan your response – which always begins with some form of agreement.

23. When a customer or colleague is being difficult and uncooperative, determine their fear and alleviate it (fear of upsetting others, fear of inaccuracies, fear of missed

deadlines, fear of being ignored). They will then be more cooperative and you can address the business issue.

24. Have a not-to-do list. To prioritize the increasingly unmanageable workloads in today's businesses, every person, team and department needs to apply the principle of focus: Focus means knowing what you *will* be doing, addressing, working on - and knowing what you *won't* be doing, addressing, working on.

25. Know your output - what results are you expected to produce? When you have done excellent work during the month, how can an observer tell? The answers to this question will be your output. Prioritize around it, and nothing else.

26. Important means "Contributes significantly to my output," and urgent means, "Needs to be done today, if it's going to be done at all." Important and urgent are not the same thing. Don't just prioritize by urgency.

27. Always consider the importance of a task or request before considering its urgency.

28. Every day, spend a chunk of time working on something that is important but not urgent.

29. Schedule important tasks (rocks) in your calendar before it gets filled with other peoples' requests and demands - then try to schedule other things around them. There is no better way to get critically important things accomplished.

30. Do your part to reduce the "cult of urgency" by asking about the business need driving urgent requests.

Summary of Tools and Skills of Customer F.I.R.S.T.

1. The 3 Things (I trust your character and competence, you clearly understand my situation, you're clearly doing all you can to help me)

2. Positive Outcome Thinking (picture events going the way you want, then planning)

3. Adversity Questions (change your thinking & be more resourceful during difficult situations)

4. Up-Front Checklist (get what's missing, verify what's there – make no assumptions)

5. Question Bridge (state the reason for the question before asking it – include a benefit)

6. Verifying Urgency (validate customer's urgency before burdening your network)

7. Paraphrasing (briefly summarize to ensure understanding)

8. S.I.P.O.C. Promise-Maker (before making commitments, be highly confident you know who is requesting, what they are requesting, who owns the process, what inputs are needed and if suppliers can deliver)

9. Can-Sandwich (when you can't give customer what they requested, first say what you can/will do, then tell them what you can't do and why, then immediately repeat what you can/will do)

10. Speech Acts (requesting, offering, declining and accepting – each act of speech has standards)

11. T.E.A.M.S. (Building action plans with suppliers: Tell them the story, enlighten each other on past wisdom, agree on a plan of action, mirror back the plan, seal the meeting)

12. Offering Options/Choices (once capacity is verified, offer 2-3 highly confident options)

13. Delivering Potentially Unpleasant News (frame it as an update, state your message neutrally, take action before contacting, if possible).

14. H.E.A.T. (hear them out – paraphrase - empathize sincerely, ask detailed questions, take action)

15. Relationship Building (ask general questions to get to know others, share a little about yourself, gradually build a relationship you both feel good about, be aware of individual and cultural differences)

16. Personality Types (speak to others from their quadrant – Ruler, Analyzer, Relater, Promoter - to reduce your differences).

17. Pain-Payoff T-chart (know your customer's priorities and concerns – then show him what he'll gain by doing the desired behavior and what he may lose by not doing the behavior)

18. Resistance Buster (anticipate objections to your request, develop counter points, then use Feel-Felt-Found, Agree-Shift-Close, etc. to frame your counterpoint)

19. Interpersonal Behaviors to Avoid (Apathy – showing indifference. Brush-off- trying to get rid of them. Coldness – showing irritation at their emotional display. Condescension – talking down to others. Rigid Robotism – resisting needed

variance. Rulebooking – hiding behind policies. Arguing – making them wrong.)

20. Forbidden Phrases ("I don't know/not my job." "You'll have to..." "We can't/you can't..." "It's not my fault." "You're wrong." "There's nothing I can do." "Let me get back to you tomorrow.")

21. The 1, 2 Punch (email and phone/voicemail in parallel to increase responsiveness, put issue and request in subject window, provide deadline and what's at stake, follow-up to place email higher in inbox)

22. The Demands Matrix (The 4 quadrants of urgency and importance, how to maximize personal productivity).

23. Schedule Rocks (Determining the proactive tasks that add the most value to the organization and scheduling them into your week).

24. Flowchart for Getting Things Done (putting it all together in one productivity system).

How The Finnamore Group Inc. Helps Companies

The Finnamore Group helps organizations through two principal types of offerings:

1. **Stand-alone training.** TFG customizes and delivers more than 40 different training modules delivered virtually or F2F on a wide range of subjects including B2B selling, customer service, collaboration, negotiation, persuasion, leading change, personal productivity, leading and managing, effective meetings, communication, etc.

   All trainings are enriched with industry- and company-specific examples and case studies and aligned to fit with the client's organizational culture.

   In addition to training, TFG also supports its client's offsites and strategic meetings with keynotes and group activities to reinforce key themes.

2. **Organizational capability-building.** TFG supports executive strategy by driving widespread, sustained behavior change that results in new organizational capabilities. This is accomplished by working with senior management as well as front line employees to change behaviors, systems/processes, and corporate culture to all become more mutually reinforcing and to achieve strategic results. Every solution is custom designed for the client's unique dynamics and needs. Following are examples of the most common (but not exclusive) types of interventions TFG implements *in addition to skills training*.

   - **Organizational sales performance.**

i. Assessment of current sales culture maturity and development of improvement strategy.

ii. Establishing/improving the sales process.

iii. Ensuring organization-wide sales support from key departments and P&Ls.

iv. Grouping sales force into performance tiers, managing each tier optimally.

v. Training sales managers to use the sales tools from the training to coach live deals.

vi. Improving proposal process lead times.

- **Customer focus / customer experience.**

  i. Assessment of current customer focus maturity and development of improvement strategy.

  ii. Reducing overpromising habits in sales team to ensure realistic customer expectations.

  iii. Improving the sales handoff process for seamless customer onboarding.

  iv. Building an internal culture of service.

  v. Overhauling the customer satisfaction assessment process for greater customer intimacy.

  vi. Driving greater customer awareness to all departments, including the shop floor.

  vii. Improving sales and operations planning processes (S&OP/SIOP).

  viii. Ensuring all decisions throughout the organization factor in customer impact.

- **Collaborative culture.**

    i. Creating an organization-wide collaboration agreement.

    ii. Improving alignment and mutual support between departments.

    iii. Reducing metric blindness through a "One Slide" strategy.

- **Continuous enterprise performance improvement.**

    i. Improving change management and continuous improvement methodologies.

    ii. Using agility hacks to improve project success.

    iii. Leveraging Beckhard-Harris equation and Kotter change process to increase buy-in.

Other Books by Brent Finnamore

The 5 Realizations of a Customer Focused Organization

Customer-Focus is becoming a priority for more and more organizations and their competitors today for a good reason - a growing body of research is showing us that improving customer service is one of the highest return on capital investments a company can make. The 5 Realizations of a Customer-Focused Organization takes you through the five realizations and their corresponding criteria for a degree of customer-focus that delivers financial results.

The first Realization, *"If I get paid, I have customers,"* begins the transition to A Culture of Service.

The second Realization, *"We must do everything from the outside-in,"* paves the way to Customer Centricity.

The third Realization, *"We must not try to satisfy everyone, it's hard enough to delight some,"* leads to Focused Excellence.

The fourth Realization, *"We cannot know our customers too well,"* is the path to Customer Intimacy.

The fifth Realization, *"Everything starts and ends with leadership,"* begins a shift to Management Support.

Each of the five criteria are detailed and shown on a five-point scale for degree of realization, giving you a complete formula and a concrete action plan for implementation.

If you're ready to turn your organization's focus from inward to outward, the proven, concise methodologies found in this book by Brent Finnamore, founder of The Finnamore Group Inc. will show you the way.

The 3-Gates Selling System

Working with thousands of top producers, Brent has captured the very best sales practices, strategies and techniques and wove them together into one seamless, practical, reproducible methodology. The 3-GATES Selling System is essential reading for B2B sales professionals, managers and executives.

Before they will buy your solution, Prospects must make three decisions; each decision is a gate in your selling process and in their buying process. The 3 gates are the three sequential challenges you must overcome with the Prospect's Buying Center - the influential team within the Prospect organization that controls the buying decision.

Gate 1 - "Why do anything at all? Why not do nothing?" They must firmly decide that they have a profit-inhibiting problem worth fixing or an opportunity worth funding.

Gate 2 - "Why this?" and "Why you?" Once they have decided to act, they must decide that your proposed solution is superior and that your firm is the best possible choice.

Gate 3 - "Why now? Why not wait?" Once they have decided to buy your solution, from you, they must feel that waiting is more expensive than acting now.

Each of these three sequential gates requires a different set of tools and skills in order to move the Prospect through their buying process and close the premium-priced deal.

In this game-changing book Brent Finnamore leverages his 25 years' experience in selling and in training and coaching sales professionals and executives around the globe to bring you the definitive formula that cracks the code for winning large, premium-priced deals.

A Culture of Collaboration

The reduced power that comes from individual people and individual departments or divisions working against one another, knowingly or not, is called *Collective Cancellation*. Each division or P&L (profit and loss center), bound by its own metrics and motives, makes it harder for the others to achieve their goals as they relentlessly drive their own. The competitive environment that emerges, combined with the lack of communication and visibility has the unintended consequence of reducing the organization's overall performance. In such an environment, *despite being given extra resources and additional incentives*, overall performance does not improve significantly, and enterprise-wide targets are missed. Furthermore, all work takes longer to complete, people miss out on the fresh perspectives of others and both time and effort are wasted trying to a) get answers to urgent questions, and b) negotiate conflicting interests. Finally, competitive interactions leave people feeling threatened, betrayed, and tired of swimming against the current, so departmental rifts widen, and silos are reinforced.

The combined power that emerges when individuals and departments focus constantly on shared metrics and motives, stay perpetually connected through clear, open communication and remain committed to putting the greater mission ahead of their individual goals might best be thought of as a *Collective Force*. It is this Collective Force that we will explore and learn how to cultivate in this breakthrough book by Brent Finnamore, president of The Finnamore Group Inc.

The World Class MRO Event Team - Dramatically improving the customer experience during product maintenance, repair and overhaul events

Maintenance, repair and overhaul organizations (MROs) are those that perform MRO services for products such as smartphones, bicycles, automobiles, heat pumps and aircraft engines. While a lot has been written about customer service, virtually nothing has been written about MRO organizations and the specific, unique implications for them when seeking to achieve customer service excellence.

When a customer sends their product for MRO service it is called an Event. In the eyes of the customer, Events are the most important interaction they will ever have with you. Events are the number one basis on which customers form their opinion of your organization and therefore the most important element of your company's value proposition. The Event is "The King of All Interactions."

The Event Team is the group of various functions that are involved in the MRO process. Event Teams are typically comprised of a front-line customer-facing function, often called customer support, along with all of the other functions involved in the Event (technicians, mechanics, finance, logistics, engineering, etc.).

PART I of this pioneering book illustrates an enormous opportunity to dramatically improve the customer's experience in the MRO enterprise by optimizing the performance of the entire Event Team. PART II examines the critical role of the Customer Event Manager (CEM) – part of the customer support function and a key member of the Event Team – and how to optimize this customer-facing role to provide world-class service.

Achieving L.I.F.T. – A complete success formula for becoming a top producer in sales

Since 1993 Brent Finnamore has inspired and motivated more than 350,000 people across the globe, empowering them to harness their personal power and reach their business and career goals. Now for the first time, Brent distills his vast experience training tens of thousands of sales professionals to bring you The L.I.F.T. Formula and enable you to become a top producer in your field.

Leverage your thoughts. How to think in ways that cause you to feel wonderful and empowered most of the time – even when things aren't going well.

Ignite your wants. How to determine what you really want and intensify your desire for it by making it clear, detailed, action-oriented and aligned with your values.

Forge deep belief. How to cultivate a feeling of certainty about your inherent ability to achieve what you want, about the excellent products and services you sell and about the great company you work for.

Take regular action. How to get yourself to take consistent, routine action - and occasionally bold action - to move you toward your clear wants and goals.

Insights – The Lessons Between the Lessons

This book is the result of 28 years of teaching between the lines. When you deliver thousands of courses, keynotes and consulting sessions to companies all over the world on a wide range of subjects like customer service, selling, teamwork, conflict, negotiation and so on, something interesting starts to happen. Everywhere you go – and I do mean everywhere – people have the same questions, regardless of the subject you're teaching or the industry you're teaching it to:

"How do you build a relationship with someone you don't like?"

"What do you do when people don't deliver on their commitments?"

"How do you deal with someone who keeps saying No and putting up resistance?"

"How do you handle someone who doesn't trust you?"

"What do you do when you have more tasks than time?"

"How do you solve a problem when every attempt fails?"

"How do you get people to want to do what you want them to do?"

"What do you do when someone blames you for everything?"

So, you try to answer these questions as best you can. Over time, through sheer repetition, you get highly practiced at answering them and your answers improve dramatically in quality and usefulness. Without meaning to consciously, you start to develop lessons between the lines – lessons within lessons. The insights that result are what form this book - applicable universally – for everyone on the planet, no matter your culture, what you do for a living, or in what industry.

www.ingramcontent.com/pod-product-compliance
Lightning Source LLC
Chambersburg PA
CBHW041313210326
41599CB00008B/256